P9-CQB-706

AN INTRODUCTION TO THE GREAT CREEDS OF THE CHURCH

BOOKS BY PAUL T. FUHRMANN

Published by The Westminster Press

An Introduction to the Great Creeds of the Church

Translated and Edited by Paul T. Fuhrmann

John Calvin's Instruction in Faith, 1537

AN INTRODUCTION TO THE GREAT CREEDS OF THE CHURCH

by

Paul T. Fuhrmann

THE WESTMINSTER PRESS

Philadelphia

LIBRARY OF CONGRESS CATALOG CARD NO. 60-10003

PRINTED IN THE UNITED STATES OF AMERICA

To

The French-speaking Protestants,
The Faculty of Theology in Paris
and
Columbia Theological Seminary
Protestant Light in Southeastern U. S.

While we are in this world, it is fitting that
we should be like birds upon the branch.
So it has pleased God, and is good for us.
—John Calvin

He hath showed thee, O man, what is good;
And what doth the Lord require of thee,
But to do justly, and to love mercy,
And to walk humbly with thy God?
—Micah 6:8

CONTENTS

FOREWORD

My colleague Dr. Paul T. Fuhrmann invites us in these pages to explore the development of the major creeds of the church by which it has confessed its faith through the centuries. With exceptional scholarly ability, he has observed the militant note of the creeds, which were born of the struggles of the church and which consequently became monuments to decisive victories.

However, as struggle has given way to victory, in all too many instances recitations of creeds have become a mere formalism, a mechanical repetition of overfamiliar words. This has created the necessity of re-examining the history of the creeds, noting the intent and meaning of these affirmations and confessions.

The words "creed," "credit," and "credulity" are formed from the same root *credo*. Rightly understood as an act of worship, the use of a creed is related more to "credit" than to "credulity," setting forth affirmations in order to give credit to God rather than to express credulity or unexamined statements of belief. In this sense, creeds are the declaration of confession and gratitude to the glory of God. Tracing the historical development, this book remarkably well demonstrates the full significance of this fact.

The struggle of the church continues. If the church can learn by its history, it must perceive the ancient creeds contextually, and be prepared to affirm its nature in open confession and gratitude through new expressions of faith in relation to the modern situation in which its present struggle is taking place. We see this recurring need demonstrated in the past, and significantly in recent history in the new French Reformed Declaration of Faith of 1936.

Dr. Fuhrmann brings this meaningful treatise to a conclusion with the pastoral consideration of the consequences of creeds and confessions of faith. The creed directs us to Scripture, and Scripture points to charity. Paul clearly affirmed the primacy of charity in our religion. In the world to come, faith and hope will cease, but charity never. Charity therefore is greater than faith and hope. (I Cor. 13:13.) The purpose of God's revelation is to create charity here on earth: "The end of the commandment is charity out of a pure heart, and of a good conscience, and of faith unfeigned" (I Tim. 1:5). "God is love; and he that dwelleth in love dwelleth in God, and God in him." (I John 4:16.) After reading such passages, how could we preach any other leading motif of God's revelation? The rediscovery of charity is the revitalization of the ancient summations of the Decalogue — love of God with the whole being, and love for neighbor as for self. When the corporate affirmation of faith and gratitude becomes a significant part of the individual, then the Christian will recognize that he lives constantly before God. The mainspring of human motivation may indeed become Christian love.

At the same time, unfortunately, the creed may still be used as an exclusive instrument for the support of intolerance and hatred. Every act of corporate worship involving the recitation of the creed without sensing the love of God necessitates a searching of one's conscience if such confession is to be meaningful.

Thomas H. McDill

Columbia Theological Seminary
Decatur, Georgia

I

CREED, SYMBOL, AND CONFESSION OF FAITH

THE PURPOSE of this book is to introduce the principal creeds by which the church, in its various ages and ways, has confessed its faith.

We use the verb "to confess" in the original sense of *confiteri* as found in the Latin Bible[1] and in Augustine's writings. When Augustine (A.D. 354–430) wrote his *Confessions,* his dominant motive and purpose was not to set forth his autobiography or to confess his former sins but to thank God and publicly praise (*confiteri*) him for what he had done for him.[2] In the creeds the church confesses its faith, that is, professes its convictions and thanks God publicly. Thus the French and other Protestants still call the creeds "confessions of faith."

Our English word "creed" comes from the Latin verb *credo,* which in Latin is the first word of the Apostles' and Nicene Creeds. Originally and etymologically, rather than "I believe," the Latin word *credo* meant primarily, "I place confidence in; I rely upon." This latter concept corresponded to the New Testament Greek word for "trust," *pistis.* When the early Christian said, *Credo in unum Deum,* he meant not so much, "I believe that a God exists," as, "I trust in one God in contrast to the many gods of paganism." Our word "creed," therefore, is related not to credulity but to credit.[3] In the creeds or confessions of faith, the Christian gives credit to God for what God has done, and declares his trust in him.

In the ancient church the creeds were called " symbols," a word derived from the language of the ancients. The Greek noun for " symbol " is related to the verb " to put together." In primitive times when a man sent a neighbor to a faraway friend, he would take an oyster shell and break it into halves, then send ahead one half of the shell to the faraway friend and give the other half to his neighbor. When the neighbor arrived at the home of the distant friend, he would present his half of the oyster shell as sign of identification. If his half fitted the half of the shell that had been sent ahead, his true identity was proved. The Greek word *symbolon* (Latin, *symbolum* or *signum*) therefore meant an object or part of an object, or later a password used for identification among members of certain religious societies.[4] In ancient Christianity, however, the word " symbol " came to mean a compendium of the fundamental facts or truths of faith that a candidate had to recite or to confirm as an evidence of his faith before being baptized and accepted as a member of the church. Now, the Apostles' or the Nicene Creed is still recited every Sunday in many churches as their standard of faith and truth.[5]

Our intention is not to offer such an extensive exposition that we will be confused by the many trees and lose sight of the forest, but rather to set forth only the dominant ideas of the principal creeds or confessions of faith, their origin, and their significance for modern Christians. People attending church services are well acquainted with the Apostles' and Nicene Creeds. But familiarity creates indifference. In other words, the constant repetition of our creeds has dulled our sensitivity, so that we have become callous to their original meaning. We shall therefore attempt to reconstruct the circumstances in which the Apostles' and Nicene Creeds were written and to exhibit their original purpose so as to regain their early forcefulness. We shall then examine a creed that has been neglected much too long, the so-called Athanasian Creed, also called, from its first two Latin words, *Quicunque vult*. We shall then consider the Waldensian Creed, the Augsburg Confession, the Gallican or La Rochelle Confession, the first draft of which was written by Calvin, and finally, the great Puritan or Westminster Confession.

It is not because we are interested in old and bygone things that we write about these creeds, but rather because these creeds or confessions of faith contain many vital elements. They can still enrich the life of the church as a whole and the inner life of Christians and non-Christians as individuals. Calvin, for example, always explained the Apostles' Creed in detail because he felt that God had deposited this treasure with the church as an aid in thinking through our faith, warming our hearts, and helping us to progress toward perfection.[6] We also think that these creeds are treasures or capital assets of the church that should be re-invested for profit, that is to say, re-examined for new values, fresh inspirations, and new motives for action.

What struck us in preparing this book was the militant note of these creeds. Paul called the Christian life a warfare (II Cor. 10:4), and compared the Christian to a soldier (I Thess. 5:8). This metaphor of Paul's became so widespread and so natural to early Christians that " soldiers of Christ " became for the early church almost a synonym for " Christians." The significance of this figure of speech was reinforced by the fact that in the western part of the Roman Empire and in Africa the Latin word for " sacrament " meant " military oath." Sharing the sacraments made all Latin-speaking Christians feel that they must be soldiers of Christ.[7]

In the light of these facts we shall see the creeds as monuments to decisive victories of the Christian faith over inner and outer enemies that in one way or another endangered its very existence. Let us not forget that Christianity in part defined and strengthened itself by way of contrast and opposition. To the narrow formalism of the Jews, Paul contrasted justification by faith without works; to the dogma of the exclusion election in Abraham of the Jewish people, Paul contrasted the election in Jesus Christ of men from all nations. Paul established Christianity through constant crises and struggles. And so it was with our creeds. It was while struggling with the secular environment and with strange doctrines that were about to alter and to suffocate Christianity that all the great creeds were written. A knowledge and study of these principal confessions of faith therefore ought to help the church in its present and future struggles.

We do not mean to say that Christianity came out of mere struggles, but rather that by its very nature the Christian faith demanded to be confessed and professed. From the very beginning, Jesus had said, " Whosoever . . . shall confess me before men, him will I confess also before my Father which is in heaven " (Matt. 10:32). Here the " I " of Jesus stands up in contrast to the whole world. And Jesus not only exacts faith but he gives the faith of God. (Mark 11:22.) Jesus is both the object and the subject (author) of faith. What is true of God is true of Christ. Here the Father and the Son are one.[8] When Jesus said, " Whosoever . . . shall confess me before men, him will I confess also before my Father which is in heaven," he established a clear connection between faith and confession of faith. The apostle Paul emphasizes their interaction: " If thou shalt confess with thy mouth the Lord Jesus, and shalt believe in thine heart that God hath raised him from the dead, thou shalt be saved. For with the heart man believeth unto righteousness; and with the mouth confession is made unto salvation " (Rom. 10:9-10). Any true faith confesses itself. And in confessing itself, it strengthens itself. The bond between faith and confession of faith is indissoluble. Acknowledging Christ as deliverer and the Lord of life involves our whole existence. It leads us to a *twofold* confession. We acknowledge our whole person, body and soul, as belonging to him. This is the confession *addressed to him* whom we love and trust, and acknowledge as Lord. This is the confession that the apostle Peter made when he said, "Thou art the Christ, the Son of the living God" (Matt. 16:16). Confession of faith involves not only the inner but also the outer or social man. Confession to be true and real must take place *before men*. It must also be addressed to them, that is, become public. "O Lord, I will confess unto thee that men also may hear," exclaimed Augustine.[9]

Confession inevitably is also decision. As the early Christian writer Tertullian (ca. A.D. 160–230) said, "Christians are not born; they become so."[10] Ancient Christian baptism well illustrates this fact. After a period of instruction in Scripture and in the tenets of the creed, the convert first turned toward the west, the land of darkness, renounced Satan, his workings and his pomp,[11] then turned toward the rising sun and confessed his allegiance to Jesus Christ.[12] This mental turning toward Jesus Christ as Lord meant turning away from all other lords. This first phase or ceremony of baptism was called abjuration or renunciation, in Latin *abjuratio* or *renuntiatio*. Then, before entering the baptismal pool, the candidate was asked these three questions: "Do you believe in God the Father Almighty?" The catechumen answered, "I believe." "Do you believe in our Lord Jesus Christ?" Answer, "I believe." And finally, "Do you believe in the Holy Spirit?" to which the answer was, "I believe." Then three times the candidate was immersed, or water was poured on his head. After he was re-dressed, his head was anointed with oil. He could then re-enter the church building and join the group of believers. At this time a second phase or ceremony called "consignment" (*consignatio*) took place: the bishop or head of the local church, placing his hands on the convert, called upon him the gift of the Holy Spirit. Thus the baptism of the Spirit followed that of water.

Once baptized, believers had to follow a still higher course of instruction about the sacraments, which are signs of the presence of Christ in his church. This course was both the summit and the completion of religious education or instruction. A Protestant historian, Prof. Marc Lods, of Paris, tells us, however, that the indispensable condition of being accepted into the ancient church was not conformity to doctrines and laws but rather a sort of initiation which Dr. Lods defines as culminating in the belief that Jesus Christ was present in his church. For early Christians, the Son of God had been made flesh, not only in his historical body while on earth, but he had also become incarnated in his mystical body, which is the church. In ancient days, Christian believers enjoyed a keen sense of the life of the church as real dispenser of the grace of God.[13] All the things we here say about ancient baptism involve faith, commitment, witnessing, and decision.

That confession was a definite decision is even more evident in the case of trials. There, Christians showed a good conscience and a serenity that was in strange contrast to their precarious situation in a pagan society. When arrested and brought before a court, Christians gave answers such as these: "My fatherland is Jerusalem," said an Egyptian martyr. "My true father is Christ, and my mother is the faith by which I believe in him," said another. "I am a slave of Christ," answered a free Roman citizen, while a slave replied, "I am a free man of Christ."[14] In courts, the question was indeed, To whom does the accused man belong?

Prof. Jean Bosc, of Paris, made us realize that Biblical texts such as I Tim. 6:12-14 and I Peter 3:15 have in their background, if not a court of justice, at least a hostile world. First Timothy 6:12-14 reads: "Fight the good fight of faith, lay hold on eternal life, whereunto thou art also called, and hast professed a good profession before many witnesses. I give thee charge in the sight of God, who quickeneth all things, and before Christ Jesus, who before Pontius Pilate witnessed a good confession; that thou keep this commandment without spot, unrebukable, until the appearing of our Lord Jesus Christ." Such a text evidently implies an unfriendly atmosphere. I Peter 3:15: "Sanctify the Lord God in your hearts: and be ready always to give an answer to every man that asketh you a reason of the hope that is in you," is a passage to be read in connection with Isa. 8:12-13, where the Lord God calls upon the prophet and his people not to fear that which the world fears and to turn away from the way of idols. Freed from the world's intolerance, Christians are here exhorted to protect themselves by giving reasons for the hope that is in them. But they can do this only by turning to Jesus Christ and confessing that they belong to him, and letting him work in them. Thus, confession of faith is a decision of man by which he, turning away from the world and its illusions, publicly confesses belonging to Christ as the only Lord, thereby avoiding the attacks of the powers of this world whatever they may be.[15]

It is thus a warfare in which the Christian is engaged and which he cannot carry on except by resting on his Lord and being strengthened by him. This third motive and meaning of confession was seen by Augustine when he said that a purpose of confession is to *stir up* the heart, that it may not sleep in despair saying, "I cannot," but awake in the love of God and be strong by his grace.[16]

The individual man is not alone in this decision and this struggle, for it is the decision and the combat of the church as a whole. Individualistic Christianity, says Professor Bosc,[17] is self-contradictory. Faith comes, indeed, from hearing the Word of God preached, and such a thing happens in the church whose mission is to preach God's Word. The believer who confesses his faith necessarily begins by confessing it to the church and in fellowship with the church. The church is in that portion of space in our universe wherein Christ is proclaimed; it is in the place where faith is declared. When a man listens to the preaching of the Word and recognizes Jesus Christ as his deliverer and his Lord, the same Spirit, which brings him to such a conviction, inserts that man into the body of Christ, which is the church, and makes him a living member of that church. The church as a whole, as a Christian community, has the responsibility for preaching. The church as a whole is called to confess its Lord with one heart and one tongue. Consequently, it is also the army that is called into combat. Undismayed by the dangers that threaten it, the church valiantly confesses before men him to whom it belongs.

The real enemies that perpetually endanger the existence and the life of the church are not its external and most manifest opponents. The reader undoubtedly recalls the saying of Tertullian's that the blood of the Christians is a seed.[18] That is to say, outright persecutions were instrumental in touching many a heart and gaining many new converts. Outer opposition has generally consolidated and strengthened the church. The real danger is when national ideologies, purely worldly methods, and local mores and ideas enter the church, settle therein, and prosper under a veneer of Christianity. When this happens, confession of faith would be the church's decision to return to its Lord, to ask itself what the substance of its faith is and should be, and in that light to draw a line between what comes from its Lord and what comes from its environment. When this differentiation is made, a great crisis is bound to occur. But crisis leads to choice, and choice leads to decision.

In order to hear the primitive voice of Christian truth and to find existential faithfulness to the Spirit of Christ, let us now turn to some ancient creeds and confessions of faith. By considering these testimonies of the church militant, we will learn to be better soldiers of Jesus Christ.

II

THE APOSTLES' CREED

"I came to bring not peace, but a sword" (Matt. 10:34), said Jesus. No epoch has better realized — that is, confirmed with facts — this prophecy of Jesus' than the two centuries that followed him.

The early Christians believed that

> "There is but one God, the Father,
>   of whom are all things,
>   and we in him;
> and one Lord Jesus Christ,
>   by whom are all things,
>   and we by him.
> For by one Spirit are we all
>   baptized into one body,
>   whether we be Jews or Gentiles,
>   whether we be bond or free;
> and have all been made to drink into one Spirit."
> (I Cor. 8:6; 12:13.)

Because of such simple faith, the early Christians had to face all sorts of persecution. As a whole the Roman officials were fair, but quite often they had to give in to the pressure of popular demand for the persecution of the Christians, which stemmed from evil rumors about them. "It is not I whom you should persuade but the people," said the Roman judge to the Christian martyr

Polycarp. In a famous rule or rescript to Pliny the Younger, then governor of Bithynia, the emperor Trajan stated practically the same policy: since they are harmless, do not seek out the Christians, but if they are denounced by the people, punish them, for such is the desire of the community.

If there was a flood, a famine, or a disastrous war, the crowds blamed the Christians and demanded that they be thrown to the lions. Just as our public officers today have to please their communities in all things, so Roman officials had to give in to public demand.[1] Thus there arose a class of early Christian writers called "apologists." They did not apologize for Christianity, but sought to defend and to vindicate it by expounding it in writing and explaining it to the authorities. Since Roman magistrates possessed a certain culture of mind and sentiments, and were generally quite reasonable, the apologists sought to present Christianity in as reasonable a light as possible.

An early apologist was Justin, who died as a Christian martyr about the year 165. He had been a philosopher and after his conversion he continued to be one because "really philosophy is a very great and very precious good in the eyes of God; when adorned with the Holy Spirit, it alone leads us toward God and unites us to him; those who apply themselves to philosophy are truly holy men."[2] Justin felt that the pagan philosophers had taught the truth in so far as they had conformed to that divine Reason or Logos which is diffused throughout the universe. Justin asserted that God, though absolute and incomprehensible, had revealed himself not only to the Jewish people[3] but to the heathens inasmuch as his Son is the divine Reason or Logos in every man. For Justin, those who have lived in conformity with truth are Christians, even though they have been mistaken for atheists.[4]

The indwelling divine Reason, which Justin identified with Christ, in the fullness of time became manifest in the flesh. In other words, the Lord Christ whom we worship is the eternal

Wisdom (Logos), the indwelling God (who fashioned the worlds and mingles with humanity as salt with the waters of the sea and as fragrance with the flowers) become incarnate. According to Justin, it is the incarnation of the Son of God that has made Christianity differ altogether from Greek philosophy. Although philosophy had no power to persuade and could not become a possession of all men, truth itself became a person in Jesus Christ and hence can be grasped by any man who believes in Him. The difference between Christianity and philosophy is a question not of quantity but of quality. As the divine Logos transcends the universe, his becoming flesh in Christ made a difference not of mere degree but of quality between our religion and Greek thought.[5] Against Jews, pagans, and persecutors, Justin defended Christianity as the only " sure and profitable " philosophy.

As Christianity spread in Greek-speaking countries, it met not only Greek philosophical traditions but also an atmosphere saturated with a sort of religion and world philosophy called Gnosticism. As a religion, Gnosticism was probably born of a combination of the Persian religion (which admitted two worlds, of good and evil, of light and darkness) with the Babylonian religion whose supreme deities were the sun, the moon, and five planets. In the Gnostic system these planetary gods were debased and made a series of emanations (aeons, that is, beings participating in both the divine and human realms or natures) more and more remote from the supreme (Persian) god of light. As a religion, Gnosticism sought both individual salvation, as the soul's deliverance from matter, and happiness after death. As a philosophy, Gnosticism arose from the perpetual question, *Pothen to kakon?* (Whence evil? What is the cause of suffering?) Compared to the infinite perfection of a supreme God,[6] the world appears indeed full of injustices, sorrows, sins, and death. How can a good God have created this evil world? The Gnostic answer was that the world in which we find ourselves is not the creation of the supreme God but the work of a Demiurge, a clumsy and inferior deity generally identified with the god of the Jews. The imagination of the Gnostics filled the gap between the supreme God and this world with a long and complicated system of increasingly weaker emanations of the divine—spirits, powers, semidivine and demonic beings. Since matter was considered utterly corrupt, the Gnostic must have no part in this lower world, but raise himself to the supreme God of light through *gnōsis*—knowledge in the sense of an ancient secret revelation, higher than reason and faith, received through initiation and perfected by ascetic discipline.[7]

Many Gnostics became members of the church. Keeping their Gnosticism as their philosophy of religion, they interpreted Christianity as if it were Gnosticism. For the Gnostics, living in a body of flesh, the soul of man was in captivity. His spiritual being was dimmed and frustrated by the material universe in which he was placed. But Christ came, a visitor from the world of pure light, to communicate a saving secret and to free the spirit of man from his bondage. Though visible to the eye, Christ was no real man, for that would imply that he was a part of the material world which is evil and far away from God. Jesus Christ therefore was but a phantom. Yet, appearing in this fashion, he was able to give the secret to his apostles, and they communicated it to their close friends.

The Gnostics distinguished two classes of men: spiritual and psychical; sometimes three classes: spiritual, psychical (soulish), and hylic (material). The spiritual alone were capable of the higher Gnostic knowledge, and hence of salvation, which was transmitted by Gnostic books, strange rites, and secret traditions reserved for a few. At the same time, Gnosticism confused Creator with creature: It conceived and represented God as *plērōma*—a fullness of existences overflowing into a multitude of lower emanations that made up a series of ever weaker entities. By giving a name to each of these perpetual divine emanations or personifications, Gnosticism founded a new mythology. For example, the Gnostics could tell all the adventures of Sophia — the divine wisdom — one of the first divine emanations who went astray to the very edge of chaos, fell into the abyss, and was finally rescued by the intervention of Christ. These poetical adventures of divine or semidivine emanations were evidently derived from paganism. Pagan influence is also reflected in the Gnostic tenet of the eternity of matter which thus became the principle of resistance to the power of God.

Certain features of Gnosticism appear contemporary. Theodotus, a disciple of Valentinus the Gnostic, taught that to possess the gnosis meant to know " what we were and what we have become; where we were and where we have been thrown; what birth is and what rebirth is." The Gnostics were anguished by their condition of being thrown into the world. They found that escaping the world was the means of conquering that once unbearable anguish. Through this gnosis, or knowledge, the individual could be saved from his body (which was a solitary confinement cell), from the visible world or sensory existence in general (which was but an immense jail).[8]

In both origin and essence, Gnosticism was foreign to the Christian church. The French Protestant historian J. Matter many years ago defined Gnosticism as " the introduction in the bosom of Christianity of all those cosmological and theosophical speculations which had formed the most considerable portion of ancient Oriental religions and had been taken over by Neoplatonists in the West." [9] Like some people today, the Gnostics had a preconceived philosophy of religion taken from their environment, and by explaining Christianity in their own terms, really did away with it.

From the very beginning Christians sensed the danger of Gnosticism. This is shown by this passage from the New Testament:

> "O Timothy, guard the deposit [10]
> abhorring the empty babbling
> and antitheses [11] of the so-called Gnosis." [12]
> (I Tim. 6:20.)

The following New Testament profession of faith was probably directed against the Gnostics:

> "God is one;
> one also the mediator between God and men,
> the man Christ Jesus,
> who gave himself a ransom for all
> as witnessed in his time." [13]
> (I Tim. 2:5-6.)

According to scholars, the following hymn or prophetic pronouncement belongs to the same class:

> "Confessedly great is the mystery of godliness:
> God was manifested in the flesh,
> justified in the Spirit,
> seen of angels,
> preached among the Gentiles,
> believed on among the world,
> received up in glory." [14]
> (I Tim. 3:16.)

A vast and subtle movement such as Gnosticism could not avoid causing powerful reactions in the church, which in several ways turned to good.

The first important gain to the church was the collection of a body of New Testament Scriptures or the formation of the New

Testament canon. The church, of course, possessed before this time inspired and authoritative writings such as the Gospels and Paul's letters. Such collections, however, had grown up informally with a view to reading and edification. But now, under pressure of the Gnostic danger, the church stressed the apostolic origin and character of these writings, erected them into a formal rule of faith and practice for the whole church. Thus toward the end of the second century grew up the definite conception of a New Testament which henceforth takes its place beside the Old Testament as of equal authority and validity with it.

Of more doubtful utility for us was a second line of defense set up in the attempt to secure a guarantee of the purity of the apostolic tradition in a continuous historical series of bishops, or episcopate, conceived of as by divine ordinance, the depository and guardian of the truth. The truth therefore was, above all, to be found in those great churches, such as Rome, Antioch, Corinth, believed to have been founded by apostles; and lists of the succession of bishops in some of the churches were carefully given in proof of the reality of this transmission of apostolic truth.

The early Christians and their writers, called church fathers, finally fell back on a third line of defense, found by them not in Greek philosophy but in what they called the "rule of faith."[15] In those days many local churches had their own creed or symbol. Other local churches adopted the creed of a nearby, more important church, which came to be the creed of most local churches of the region. We know several of these creeds or symbols belonging to the churches of Rome, Jerusalem, Antioch, Caesarea in Palestine, and Alexandria, which were important in ancient Christianity.

Originally, the creed was a brief formula used at baptism (as we saw in Chapter I) when the convert was received into the church after reciting or answering the question, Do you believe . . . ? with such words as[16]

"I believe in God the Father,
in the Son Christ,
in the Holy Spirit.
I believe in the remission of sins
and eternal life
through the holy church."

We know the creed used in Rome. This ancient Roman creed, which was the forerunner of our Apostles' Creed, had existed since about the year 150.[17] It said:

"I believe in God the Father Almighty;
And in Christ Jesus, his only Son, our Lord,[18]
who was born of the Holy Spirit and Mary the Virgin,
who under Pontius Pilate was crucified and buried;
the third day, he rose from the dead,
ascended to the heavens, sat down at God's right hand,
whence he will come to judge the living and the dead;
And in the Holy Spirit, the holy church, the remission of sins
and the resurrection of the flesh."

Scholars such as Harnack, Loisy, Lietzmann, and Kelly [19] thought its earlier skeleton to have been:

"I believe in God the Father Almighty
And in Jesus Christ, his only Son, our Lord,
And in the Holy Spirit, the holy church,
the resurrection of the flesh."

The French scholars J. Lebreton and A. Loisy thought that this basic formula was the result of a threefold interrogation on the baptismal command found in Matt. 28:19: "Go ye therefore, and teach all nations, baptizing them in the name [that is, by the power] of the Father, and of the Son, and of the Holy Spirit." An evidence of this truth is the fact that E. Hauler found and published in 1900 long fragments of a Latin version of an ancient liturgical document where baptism is described. Other scholars [20] traced these Latin fragments to the "apostolic tradition" which Hippolytus of Rome (ca. A.D. 170–235) had written down in Greek. One may read there that, before baptizing them, the presbyter asked catechumens three questions on faith as following:

> "[Do you believe in God the Father Almighty?]
> Do you believe in Christ Jesus, the Son of God,
> who was born of [*de*] the Holy Spirit out of [*ex*] Mary the Virgin,
> and was crucified under Pontius Pilate, dead and buried,
> and on the third day resurrected alive [*resurrexit . . . vivus*] from the dead,
> and ascended in heaven,
> sits at the right hand of the Father
> [and] is to come to judge the quick and the dead?
> Do you believe in the Holy Spirit
> and the Holy Church
> and the resurrection of the flesh?"

In order to understand the Apostles' Creed, scholars such as P. Nautin therefore no longer stop at the old Roman creed but go farther back to Hippolytus' apostolic tradition, so that the interpretation of the original meaning of the Apostles' Creed given by K. Holl and A. Harnack needs to be revised. Resting on the old Roman creed, K. Holl had noticed that the words "Christ Jesus" were followed by two titles: "Only Son" and "Our Lord." Holl took the words "who was born of the Holy Spirit and Mary the Virgin" to be an explanation of the title "Only Son" and the words "who under Pontius Pilate was crucified and buried; the third day, he rose from the dead, ascended to the heavens, sat down at God's right hand, whence he will come [*venturus*] to judge the living and the dead" as explaining the title "Lord." Holl relied on the old Roman creed as if it had been composed all at once and in one sitting. The fact is that the apostolic tradition offers a more ancient form of the creed where the title " Our Lord " does not appear. Since the title " Our Lord " was lacking in this older form, its users and readers could attribute the title " Son of God " only to the virgin birth, which followed immediately the title " Son of God."

What P. Nautin said about Holl, he said also about Harnack. Starting from Holl's statements, Harnack had suggested the following complete scheme of the architecture of the creed:

God	Father	Almighty
Jesus Christ	Son	Lord
Holy Spirit	Holy Church	[Remission of sins and] [21] resurrection of the flesh

Harnack had taken the three members of each line as expressing identities (*Identitätgleichung*), the three members of each column as corresponding to one another so as to form a thematic (the first) column, a revelation (the second) column, and a force-effect (the third) column. P. Nautin was unable to see Harnack's identity between Spirit, church, and resurrection of the flesh. The creed in the apostolic tradition suggested to him a different relationship between these three terms. Not only so, but Nautin claimed that the absence of the words " our Lord " in the more ancient apostolic tradition destroyed all the " theological geometry " of Professor Harnack. Thus, he put forward a different general understanding of the creed, historical rather than theological, as follows: [22] The Christian writers of the first centuries did not understand the names Father, Son, and Holy Spirit as these are misunderstood today. When reading these names, modern men immediately think of three Persons existing eternally, independent of creation and redemption. In other words, and using a later theological language, modern readers place themselves at the outset in the order (or later theology) of *processions,* which, as we shall see in Chapter IV, Augustine worked out only several centuries later than the apostolic tradition. The early church writers saw in the Father the "Creator of heaven and earth"; in the Son they saw Jesus born of a virgin; and in the Holy Spirit, the grace (*charis*) of the Christian principle of life and resurrection. They were in what Nautin calls the order of *missions*. And, in the imaginative representation that accompanies all languages, the Father was localized above all things; the Son, "at the right hand of the Father . . . , [whence] he shall come to judge the quick and the dead"; the Holy Spirit, within us Christians.[23] The Trinity was thus originally thought and understood through the mystery of our salvation. This was the general perspective of that age, and it is that of the Apostles' Creed. It was already the perspective of the Scripture in Luke 1:35: "The virtue of the Most High will cover you Mary with his shadow; *it is why* the Holy Being which will be born of you will be called Son of God," and in John 7:39: "The Spirit was not yet."[24] Is not this the spontaneous way of ancient Christians and the natural road to a truly Christian understanding of our creed? Was not Christianity a mystery and was not that Christian mystery essentially a life in Jesus Christ?[25]

According to this primitive way of understanding the Trinitarian formula, the Holy Spirit was, above all, seen in his function of life of the Christian. But, following the more explicit teaching of the Johannine Christ, as this life is conferred through Baptism and Eucharist (which are at the same time acts of the church and initiation into the church), it was perfectly consistent to say that the Spirit is in the church, and the mention of the Spirit in the third baptismal question by itself suggested the church. The necessity to stop heresies was only the occasion to pay attention to this essential bond which existed between Spirit and church and which tended to bring the two together.[26]

In comparing all the different creeds of the other ancient

churches, we find them to have been quite similar: their skeleton was generally the same; that is, they had three articles corresponding to the three Persons of the Trinity; they generally enumerated the principal events of the life of Jesus Christ — his birth, suffering, death, resurrection, and ascension to heaven from which he shall come. The only explanation of the similarity is that in meeting Gnostic errors it was felt necessary to add to the brief creed used at baptism (hence called Baptismal Creed) certain statements against Gnostic teachings. Thus another consequence of the struggle with Gnosticism was that each expanded creed came to be considered as an actual *rule* for faith, a kind of legal document. Its purpose was to set forth clearly what the church believed in opposition to the Gnostics. And this was done by means of a few carefully chosen phrases every word of which was there for a definite reason. Thus the symbols or creeds came to be truly rules of faith, standards of the truth, and distinctive signs of Christianity.

The Apostles' Creed that we recite in church today is simply an expansion of the ancient Roman creed, which we have given above. Our Apostles' Creed was originally the barrier that the church erected against Gnosticism.

The Gnostics were so impressed with the magnitude and number of the evils and miseries of this world that they denied the oneness, goodness, and almightiness of God. Our creed affirms that "I believe in God"; that is, I have confidence in God in contrast to the many vain gods of the heathens and aeons of the Gnostics; I trust him as *the almighty* [27] *Father* of the universe revealed in Jesus, not only but also as the ultimate author of the things stated in this creed, which is a sum of the history of our salvation from creation to the end of time. Filled with a despairing pessimism and contempt for this world, the Gnostics denied that God could have been its creator. The creed affirms that God is the "Maker of heaven and earth," the Creator of all things.

The ultimate subject of my faith is God, yet he remains a mystery until the Last Day, when I shall see him face to face in his final Kingdom. The Gnostics had a long line of intermediary aeons that separated God from men. The creed affirms one intermediary, Jesus Christ. The Gnostics, after all, denied the divinity of Christ inasmuch as they believed in several divine aeons. The creed affirms Jesus Christ to be the " only [28] Son " of God " our Lord." The Gnostics spread the notion that our Deliverer did not have a real body, a true humanity and historicity, having been a mere phantom on earth. The creed affirms that Jesus Christ, " conceived by the Holy Spirit," [29] was truly " born of " a human mother whose name is even preserved in history — Mary the Virgin.

The Gnostics denied that Christ had really suffered and died. The creed fixes the very time that he " suffered " by giving the exact name of the Roman procurator in Judea, which was at that time " under Pontius Pilate." The Gnostics believed that redemption derived from gnosis, that is, a previous revelation or higher knowledge only transmitted by Christ. The creed insists that our redemption comes from that efficacy found in the very death of Jesus Christ. Our creed indeed affirms that Jesus Christ was " crucified," really " died," and was even " buried," asserting what every early Christian believed, that is, that Jesus Christ " descended into hell," the abode of the dead, in order to share our common lot, yet to complete his triumph over the dominion of sin and death, and to preach the gospel to Jews and pagans who had died before his coming.[30] The Gnostics, who believed in evolutions of the soul, also, with others, denied a final resurrection. Our creed states that Christ " rose again from the dead." Certain Gnostics held that the Christ who ascended to heaven was a mere spiritual being without a real human body. The creed affirms that Christ with his body " ascended into heaven " (past tense) and at this very moment " sitteth " (present tense) as supreme power " on the right hand of God the Father Almighty," which means that Christ went triumphantly through all the spheres of reality (hell, earth, heaven), reaching the right side of God, that is, that very condition in which God is. Certain Gnostics believed that, as the human soul evolves continually, there was no need for a Last Judgment. The creed, however, proclaims that "from thence he [Jesus Christ] shall come" (future tense) "to judge the quick and the dead." The work of Jesus Christ is complete. It takes in the past, the present, and the future.

The Gnostics believed in human and other spirits of all sorts. The creed affirms that you and "I believe in the *one* Holy Spirit." The Gnostics and others had established a swarm of sects, little conventicles and spurious societies. The creed sets forth the uniqueness of "the holy catholic [31] church," which is related to the Holy Spirit and belongs to God and not to man, "the communion of saints." [32] Certain celibate and perfectionist sects had their own rigoristic views about remission of sins. The creed proclaims the validity of the church's system of public penance for "the forgiveness of sins" through the mediation of the holy church. The Gnostics, despising the flesh, did not believe in a final resurrection of the body. Our creed affirms the redeemability of human nature (the flesh) to be fully manifested at the end, and proclaims "the resurrection of the body" and "life everlasting." [33] No Gnostic would have accepted these additions. And the creed thus withstood the Gnostics victoriously.

Some might think that the Apostles' Creed is defective inasmuch as it does not say that Jesus has atoned for our sins. But the atonement is implicit in the facts set forth by the creed. Is the theological question, "How did Jesus atone for men's sins?" a real problem? Could not Jesus' appearance among men and his death be considered not a cause but an effect of the approach of God's Kingdom? Are not Christ's coming, death, and resurrection a revelation of God's love, and evidence, sign, and proof that

God's love is infinite and saves us? [34] Is not the creed a sum of the history of our salvation reaching from creation to the end of time?

The time of Gnosticism was also a time of persecution. The Roman State's attack from without and the insidious Gnostic peril within helped and indeed compelled the Christian communities to gather around their bishops [35] as trustees of the true apostolic tradition and representatives of Jesus Christ, and to realize that they formed the holy church which shall never perish from the earth. And so it came that to this day we consciously and forcefully say:

"I believe in God the Father Almighty,
Maker of heaven and earth;
And in Jesus Christ his only Son our Lord;
who was conceived by the Holy Ghost,
born of the Virgin Mary,
Suffered under Pontius Pilate,
was crucified, dead, and buried;
he descended into hell;
the third day he rose again from the dead;
He ascended into heaven,
and sitteth on the right hand of God the Father Almighty;
from thence he shall come to judge the quick and the dead.
I believe in the Holy Ghost; the holy catholic church;
the communion of saints;
the forgiveness of sins;
the resurrection of the body;
and the life everlasting. Amen."

III

THE NICENE CREED

The Gnostics had said that Christ was not truly human, that he was a mere phantom or apparition by means of which the Son of God made himself visible to men. The question next arose, What do we really mean when we say that Jesus Christ is the Son of God? Was he truly God? This inquiry was of far-reaching importance and very difficult to answer. The ancient creeds or symbols were Trinitarian, that is, they affirmed faith in the Father, in the Son, and in the Holy Spirit. But the relationship existing among the three, especially the relationship between the Father and the Son, constituted a problem. The names Father and Son had been taken from family life. But what exactly did they mean? How was the expression "Son of God" to be understood? In Christ there is a divine nature and a human nature as well, but how does that divine nature come forth from the nature of God?

In the second and third centuries, Christian teachers gave two opposite general answers:

1. Wishing to safeguard at all costs the oneness of God, that is, complete monotheism or faith in only one God, some teachers emphasized God the Father, hence lessening the dignity of the Person of Christ. These teachers were called "monarchists" or "monarchians" because they were boldly defending the "monarchy"[1] or sole government of God versus polytheism. They resolved the Person of Christ into the first Person alone, that of

God the Father Almighty. Consequently, they neglected the importance of the Son. Though their starting point was the same, that is, to assure total monotheism, the monarchians offered two incompatible solutions:

a. The first is called adoptionism: only God the Father is God; Jesus Christ was not his Son by nature but only by adoption; he was a man like all other men; God, however, especially chose him and invested him with his power at the moment of baptism by declaring, " Today have I generated thee."[1] The Spirit of God came on him that day, and he was filled with the Spirit to a degree higher than were other men. In this way the adoptionist explanation safeguarded the monarchy of God the Father Almighty.

b. Sabellianism was the second monarchian theory or solution. It was so called from Sabellius, its most eminent representative: God the Father alone is God; Jesus Christ is only a body in which God the Father incarnated himself, that is, came in the flesh among men. God the Father is the only divine Person. The Son is not a distinct Person.[2] Ultimately, the Son is only an aspect, another mode or way of being of the perfectly one God. God the Father has accomplished our redemption all by himself. It is the Father who came in the flesh, who suffered and was put on the cross.

These two opposite monarchian doctrines, adoptionism and Sabellianism, starting from the same base, denied all essential distinctions within the Godhead.[3] In these doctrines, the Son has no personality. He remains without color and substance, consequently useless in the plan of God's salvation. Hence adoptionism and Sabellianism were rejected and officially condemned by the church at the end of the second and the beginning of the third century.

2. Other church teachers disagreed with the monarchians. Wishing to give to Jesus Christ the place and rank that he deserves,

they divided the divinity or deity in two. This second current of theological thinking was represented by Origen, a brilliant teacher in the third century. Origen taught that the Son is God[4] along with and beside God the Father, divided from and inferior to him.[5] The Son is a second-grade God,[6] issued from the Father but below him and by nature different from the Father. In a recently discovered work of Origen, we may read these categorical formulas: Christ is "different from the Father,"[7] and more clearly still, "We confess two gods."[8]

There can be no doubt about the thought of Origen: the Son is other than the Father; he is not of the same substance or nature of the Father because his nature is somehow intermediate and intermediary between God and men. As Origen had a considerable prestige and following, he was not officially condemned, but his position in theology was criticized by many. One of these critics was Dionysius of Rome, who stood sharply against the opinions of Bishop Dionysius, pupil and successor of Origen in the school of Alexandria. This "quarrel of the two Dionysiuses" is important in the unfolding of the church's thinking about the Trinity. The Dionysius of Rome had had his schooling in Greece. As he was elected bishop of Rome (A.D. 259), he came to share the Western idea of the consubstantiality of the Trinity, which Tertullian had formulated and put into circulation in the Western part of the Empire.

The first writer whom we think to have used the word "Trinity" almost in our sense was Theophilus of Antioch about the year 175 when he taught that "the first three days of Creation are types of the Trinity (Greek, *trias*)."[9] Then the word was used by Clement of Alexandria and by Origen. But Tertullian was the first to use our words "Trinity," "three Persons," "one Substance" (*Trinitas, tres Personae, una Substantia*), and wrote of the Son and the Holy Spirit as deriving from the substance of the Father.[10] Cyprian and Novatian immediately adopted this usage.

Dionysius of Alexandria objected to the word "consubstantial" (Greek, *homoousios*) because it was new and unknown to sacred writers, but finally he consented to its use to indicate, however, not the identity or sameness but the affinity between the essence of the Son and the essence of the Father, and to distinguish the Son from creatures or created beings.

In the meantime the number of Jewish converts, who once were the guardians of monotheism, greatly decreased in the church. The majority of Christians, in the West especially, now equated freely the Son and the Father. Up to this time no official pronouncement had been made in the church on this question, but then suddenly a great controversy about Arius broke out among Christians.

A few extant fragments[11] permit us to reconstruct objectively the thought of Arius: He desired to save monotheism and the transcendence of the only one, ungenerated, and eternal God. To speak of generation would have been attributing a change to God; the possibility that God had communicated his essence would imply that such essence is not simple but compound and divisible; to speak of a oneness of divine substance in both the Father and the Son would be affirming either a philosophical absurdity or two gods. Therefore, the Son was an intermediary between God and the world, and to this end the Word[12] had been created from nothing[13] before the world, for originally nothing existed except God.

The thought of Arius to a large extent had been influenced by ancient Greek philosophy. Modern man believes in an expanding economy and expects profits to pile up out of all proportion to the original investment. In philosophy and science we can therefore easily imagine an ever-expanding and self-renewing universe. It is easy for moderns to think of an effect or product as being superior to its cause or maker. But it was an axiom with the ancient Greeks that an effect or product is always weaker and lower than its cause or maker. Hence, for them, God could not have created something superior or even equal to himself. The Son could not possibly be equal to the Father. For Arius, the Son was created before all creation and before all times,[14] yet he was a creature. The Son was not of the substance of the Father and not even similar to him. The Son was not eternal, since he had had a beginning, and to think that he existed before being begotten was an absurdity.

The philosophically minded clergy suspected that Arianism was a turning, if not to Gnosticism, certainly to a sort of Neoplatonic emanationism. The educated class of pagans at this time, though no longer believing in fables and myths, still maintained paganism philosophically. "What is eternally perfect eternally generates; what is generated is eternal but inferior to the generating principle."[15] The intelligible and sensible world is eternally begotten through degradation from a supreme Principle, source of all that which is and will be. All things receive their reality from the divine One through intermediary entities and personal deities. All things are intelligible because they all proceed from a higher Intelligence. Hence happiness consists in intellectual activity. The purpose of life and philosophy is a mystical return of the soul to the supreme God. This was the teaching and message of the Neoplatonists. And Christians feared that Arianism would turn out to be a form of emanationism. That is, they felt that if the Son of God were debased, his entire creation would become debased, and all philosophical categories of being would become degraded as a result.

The more Evangelical clergy looked upon Arius as undermining the certainty of our redemption. They felt that only God, by becoming man, can lift up humanity to God.

The practical-minded clergy and Christians in positions of responsibility also did their bit of reasoning. They argued that if Arius teaches the existence of two gods, why not teach the existence of many gods, as the heathen did? Was not Arius, then, opening a door for the return of paganism? If there were more than one God, there would be more than one morality. What pleases one god might indeed displease another god, and the result would be moral chaos all over the Empire. Then what of the balance between Caesar and Christ? If Arius lowered the Lord of the church, then in effect he raised the prestige of Caesar, lord of the Empire. Raising up the state meant lowering the church. Finally, those in Alexandria who were bent upon protecting its prestige as a center of learning and caring for its good reputation resisted the Arian heresy, and this time the very bishop of Alexandria turned against his priest Arius. The controversy rapidly spread throughout the East and the entire church was divided.

By this time Constantine had become emperor. He had hoped to get much help from the Christian church in his great task of unifying and governing the immense Empire. Finding the church to be sharply divided, he resolved to summon from all over the territory occupied by the Empire a council of the whole church. The Council met at Nicaea, a city not far from Constantinople, in May and June, 325. It came to be called the first ecumenical council. In those days, when men's minds were not affected by an expanding world as today, the word "ecumenical" did not mean "world-wide" but simply "of the Empire." The emperor came to open the Council. Two hundred and twenty [16] bishops were present. The purpose of the Council was to find a formula that would state unmistakably and fully what the church believed about the Lord Jesus Christ. If this formula were found, it would bring peace and unity to the church, and the church would solidify the Empire.

The great question then was, Is the Son Very God of Very God? Is he truly and completely divine, or was he, as the Arians imagined, a subordinate being, divine but not with the same divinity of God the Father? As the debate went on, the Greek word *homoousios* became the word of contention. The word was well chosen. Made of two words, *homo* (of the same) and *ousia*[17] (substance), the term expressed two subtle philosophical concepts: identity of substance, and yet plurality of persons. The word " consubstantial " can be applied to two beings only if they are distinct. One thing can not be consubstantial with itself alone. A thing can be consubstantial only with another thing. Hence, there must be a plurality of divine persons who yet are of the same substance.[18] Our prefix *con-* means indeed " in company with." But the Arians would not accept the *homoousios* or " *con*-substantial." The semi-Arians might have accepted *homoiousios* (of like substance) — a vague word that would have left everything indefinite.

To solve the problem, the Council took an already existing creed or symbol as a skeleton for a new one. Some scholars think that this skeleton was the creed of the church in Caesarea; others think it was the creed of the church in Jerusalem. In any case, it was a short creed with a general pattern similar to our Apostles' Creed. The Council added certain statements to that existing creed so as to settle the matter. Against a recurrence of emanationism, the Council added to the first article about " God, . . . Maker of all things," the words " visible and invisible "[19] and made it read: " We believe in one God the Father Almighty, Maker of all things *visible and invisible*." Against Arius, the Council made the second article say, " And in one Lord Jesus Christ the son of God, *only-begotten Son of the Father, that is to say, of the substance*[20] *of the Father,* God of God, Light of Light, *true God of true God, begotten not made, of one same substance with the Father;* through whom all things were made, *things in heaven*[21] *and things on earth;* who for us men and for our salvation *came down,* was made flesh, *and became man,* suffered and rose again on the third day and ascended into heaven and is to come to judge the living and the dead; and in the Holy Spirit."[22]

By using the word "substance" twice in this creed, the Council affirmed its position against the Arians. All the members of the Council, except two, signed this creed.

All seemed well. But shortly the dispute broke out worse than ever. Constantine, the emperor, changed his mind. He and his successors generally came to back the Arian or semi-Arian party. Like all religious contention, this dispute was mixed up with political, racial, and social questions. As the cities were rivals, Constantinople in a spirit of contentiousness was apt to become Arian for the only reason that Alexandria was orthodox. The whole church was again divided.

The great opponent of Arianism was Athanasius, who was born in Alexandria about 296. He was a little man, so small that his opponents called him a dwarf. We all remember the saying, "Athanasius against the world"—*Athanasius contra mundum*. His name, however, stands for those who resist not only society but the church itself in the interest of some higher truth which it has not yet understood and appreciated.

Athanasius had a sort of metaphysical certainty: if the Son and the Spirit were created entities, we men through them would have no contact with God. We would be united to the Son and to the Spirit as created things to created things, and we would still be alien to the divine nature.[23] But the incarnation, that is, God becoming flesh, created a different and higher humanity than ours. The incarnation is not a lessening of the Divinity. It is a lifting up of man, making him godlike.[24] For half a century Athanasius defended the redemption and new dignity of man against all assailants. At times, Arianism seemed likely to win. It gained much popular support. To profess Arianism was to exhibit intellectual culture. The leaders of Arianism had generally been nurtured on profane antiquity. They were the successors of the rhetoricians and sophists. Endowed with a superabundance of words and fallacious erudition, they were able to sway superficial and easily changed people. The crowds were flattered to be called upon to participate in working out a deep question in theology. Arianism was presented in songs and jokes for the use of the masses, who now would transform the *homoousios* of Nicaea into the *homoiousios,* thus denying the Trinity, and change the generation (*gegennēmenos*) of the Son into his creation (*gegenēmenos*), thus denying his divinity. As Arianism was a pagan reaction, it gained the support of worldly people who disliked the authority of the Christian church.

Arianism was a weak and tamed form of Christianity offering little resistance to the ambition of the state. This tamed form of Christianity gained the favor of the imperial court with its immense power. Unable to distinguish very well the rights of God and those of Caesar, the Arian clergy was generally full of respect toward the imperial purple. This explains why Arianism became acceptable to emperors and was patronized by the early successors of Constantine as their true form of Christianity. But students know that the reality of Constantine's conversion to Christianity is still a subject of discussion.

In any case the Empire itself had not been converted. The old pagan principle was still alive. The idea of the divinity of the state was the very soul of the Empire. Its corollary or logical consequence was the almightiness of the sovereigns. They aimed to keep their authority over all minds and to regulate the whole life of society. Since the time of Diocletian (284–305), everything that touched the person of the emperor was called "divine" or "sacred." And so men spoke of the "sacred palace" and "sacred bedchamber" of the emperor. The single conversion of Constantine could scarcely have changed the mentality of the rulers. Their imperial minds were not yet able to see a distinction between the pagan political principle that the bodies and souls of people belong to the state and the Christian principle of the sacredness of human conscience. The emperors never doubted for an instant that they had the same rights over the new Christian religion that they had had over the former pagan religion. The idea of a spiritual society or church independent of the state is a modern idea. The ancient emperors considered the church as a part of the state and hence subject to their orders. " My will takes the place of church regulations," was the emperor's answer to the prelates who quoted to him the laws of the church.[25] These words of the ruler were the faithful application of the principle of law as stated by the great lawyer Ulpian: " What pleases the prince has the force of law " (*Quod principi placuit legis habet vigorem*). To people and emperors this principle was a legal dogma and beyond question, just as the American Constitution is to the American people and their presidents.

What we have just said accounts for the early Christian emperors' attitude toward the church. They considered themselves a kind of lay pope with the duty of looking after the interests of the church. They acted in good faith and felt entitled to dictate their policies to the church. Thus when Athanasius stood by the Nicene Creed, he stood for the independence and freedom of the church even when the church did not appreciate or want them. Five times Athanasius was banished from his diocese or had to escape into exile. While many faltered, and many doubted, Athanasius stood firm; and if the faith of Nicaea won the day at last, it was largely due to him.[26]

Weary of struggles, the church finally assembled into a second ecumenical council at Constantinople in 381. It unanimously endorsed the decision of Nicaea. But in the course of years, the churches that had remained faithful to the Nicene Creed felt a need to harmonize the Nicene Creed with the Apostles' Creed, which had become the Confession of Faith in the Western part of the Empire. Consequently, the following expressions in italics were taken from the Apostles' Creed and inserted into that of Nicaea:

God creator *of heaven and earth;*
The Son was incarnated *by the Holy Spirit in the bosom of Mary the Virgin;*
He was crucified *under Pontius Pilate;*
He ascended to heaven *and sitteth at the right hand of the Father.*

Since Marcellus of Ancyra denied that Christ's reign would continue after the Day of Judgment, the clause " of whose Kingdom there shall be no end " was added.[27]

And since the so-called Pneumatomachists (" enemies of the Spirit "), Macedonians and Marathonians (so called from the names of their leaders), thought with the Arians that the Spirit was a mere created being or creature, the need was felt to expand the third article on the Holy Spirit. The Nicene Council had simply asserted that you and " I believe in the Holy Spirit." But the letters of Athanasius to Serapion (A.D. 356–362) and the large treatise of Basil on the Holy Spirit (375) show a growing appreciation of the Spirit's divinity and work. The incarnation made possible the life of the Spirit: the Holy Spirit leads men to participate in that life which is in God. The Holy Spirit acts on all men, but he dwells only in those who have been renewed after the image of God who created them. The churches that had remained faithful to Nicaea agreed to recite the following words about the Spirit as " the Lord, and Vivifier, who proceeds from the Father, worshiped and glorified with the Father and the Son, who has spoken through the prophets."

All these developments were introduced little by little. A letter in Epiphanius' The Firmly Anchored Man, dated 374, gives us practically the complete expanded text that we recite today under the name of Nicene Creed. This expanded form of the Nicene Creed was not discussed at the Council of Constantinople in 381. It was the Council of Chalcedon in 451 that officially adopted the text expanded by the Eastern churches.

To be complete, we should add a few words about the so-called filioque, "and from the Son." The expanded text of Nicaea, which was accepted and endorsed at Chalcedon in 451, said that the Holy Spirit proceeded from the Father. Cyril of Alexandria, who was made patriarch of that city in 412, taught that the Spirit proceeds from the Father through the Son. This became the interpretation of the Greek-speaking or Eastern part of the church. The church in the Western part of the Empire followed Augustine, who taught that the Spirit proceeds from the Father *and from the Son—procedit a patre filioque.* As early as 447 some Latin churches squarely introduced this filioque, "and from the Son," in their recitation of the Nicene Creed. Thus a serious dispute arose between Greek and Latin Christians. The Greeks thought that to introduce, without the decision of an ecumenical council, even one single new word into the Nicene Creed was a grave infidelity and to this day they have not accepted the filioque. The Latins, on the other hand, thought that the filioque expressed more correctly the data of the Bible. This was one of the causes of the final separation of the Greek and Latin churches in 1054.

Let us sum up and yet distinguish four steps in the making of the so-called Nicene Creed as recited today:

1. At Nicaea in 325, a first text was accepted and was endorsed by the Council at Constantinople in 381.

2. This text was expanded in the Eastern churches with additions from the Apostles' Creed and with new data about the Holy Spirit. This expanded text existed before the Council of Constantinople (381), which, however, did not consider it.

3. The Council of Chalcedon in 451 officially accepted and endorsed the expanded form of the creed.

4. The churches in the West and the Synod of Toledo in 589 officially added the filioque; and hence it comes that today we

still recite this so-called Nicene Creed which, properly speaking, should be called the Chalcedonian Creed or the Niceno-Chalcedonian Creed:

"I believe in one God the Father Almighty,
Maker of heaven and earth,
and of all things visible and invisible:
And in one Lord Jesus Christ, the only-begotten Son of God;
begotten of his Father before all worlds,
God of God,
Light of Light,
Very God of Very God;
begotten, not made;
being of one substance with the Father;
by whom all things were made:
who for us men and for our salvation came down from heaven,
and was incarnate by the Holy Ghost of the Virgin Mary,
and was made man:
and was crucified also for us under Pontius Pilate;
He suffered and was buried:
and the third day he rose again according to the Scriptures:
and ascended into heaven,
and sitteth on the right hand of the Father:
and he shall come again, with glory, to judge both the quick and the dead;
whose kingdom shall have no end.
And I believe in the Holy Ghost, the Lord, and Giver of Life,
who proceedeth from the Father and the Son;
who with the Father and the Son together is worshiped and glorified;
who spake by the Prophets:

And I believe one Catholic and Apostolic Church:
I acknowledge one Baptism for the remission of sins:
And I look for the Resurrection of the dead:
and the Life of the world to come. Amen."

We have given the creed as recited in the Anglican Church and in most churches today. May we add a few general remarks on this Nicene (more accurately Niceno-Chalcedonian) Creed?

1. This creed is far more doctrinal and philosophical than the Apostles' Creed. As the reader recalls, the reason is that it was a statement to stop Arianism, and an instinctive reaction against Neoplatonic emanationism.

2. This creed was probably introduced into the Roman churches when the Byzantine emperor Justinian reconquered Italy from German tribes in 535 and strove to submit the whole church to his authority. The Creed was unable to supplant, as in the Greek churches, the Apostles' Symbol or Creed, but in the West it probably pushed aside the old Roman or Apostles' Creed to the position of Baptismal Creed.

3. This creed is the only truly ecumenical creed, that is to say, it is accepted and recited by all Christian churches: Greek Orthodox, Roman Catholic, and all major Protestant denominations.[28]

4. The Nicene Creed declares Jesus Christ to be not only consubstantial with the Father but also consubstantial with us because he was perfect in his divinity and perfect in his humanness. He is the one and same Savior in two natures, without change, without division and without separation. This union does not suppress the distinction of the two natures. On the contrary, each nature keeps its proprieties, yet the two natures are united in one person. There is no Christ divided into two persons but one only Son—the Divine Word or Logos—our Lord and King,[29] Jesus Christ.

IV

THE ATHANASIAN CREED OR QUICUNQUE VULT

IN HIS MONK'S CELL at Bethlehem in the year 410, Jerome had begun to dictate his Commentary on Ezekiel when the news came that the city of Rome had fallen into the hands of Alaric the Goth. " My mind was so upset," he writes, " that, as the saying is, I could not remember my own name. For a long time I did not speak a word. I knew that this was a time for tears." [1] With the fall of Rome, all culture of mind and sentiment in the West fell. For more than a century, armed bands of barbarians traversed all parts of the West sacking the cities that Hellenic genius and Roman patience had erected, destroying monuments, killing or taking the peasants captive. The expiring Empire became an easy prey to all kinds of barbarians. The Vandals left so clear a memory of their work that after fifteen hundred years, the word " vandalism " still means the passion for senseless destruction. The Huns, repulsive and scarcely human horsemen from Tartary, said that the grass never grew again on the soil touched by the hoofs of their horses.

Many cities were razed to the ground and were never rebuilt; others fell to the rank of villages. The splendid system of roads and posts,[2] the theaters, the magnificent social centers that were public baths and courts, all gradually fell to ruin. There were no public schools, no drama, no literature, no art. Everything was tottering and sinking. Society was in dissolution. In the West there was no art, no philosophy, and no theology. In the early years of the sixth century, Caesarius, bishop of Arles in Provence, rubbed elbows with great and rich merchants who were unable to read and much less to write. Fifty years later, concern for general culture had disappeared in Gaul. A book was an extreme rarity. The very few persons who still claimed to be scholars were able to read only a few verses from the Bible and to draw up some official deed or document by copying it from a book of prescribed forms! [3] The majority of Christians believed that the last age of the world had come. It was the night of the spirit and the death of a world.

Everything was at its lowest ebb, everything seemed without hope, when suddenly out of Gaul arose this magnificent Confession of unshakable Faith:

"Whosoever earnestly desires to be saved must above all hold the Catholic Faith. Which Faith unless every one do keep whole and undefiled, without doubt he shall perish in eternity. And the Catholic Faith is this:

"I. That we worship one God in Trinity, and Trinity in Unity; neither confounding the Persons: nor dividing the Substance. For there is one Person of the Father, another of the Son: and another of the Holy Ghost. But the Godhead of the Father, of the Son, and of the Holy Ghost is all one: the Glory equal, the Majesty coeternal. Such as the Father is, such is the Son: and such is the Holy Ghost. The Father uncreated, the Son uncreated: and the Holy Ghost uncreated. The Father incomprehensible, the Son incomprehensible: and the Holy Ghost incomprehensible. The Father eternal, the Son eternal: and the Holy Ghost eternal. And yet they are not three eternals: but one eternal. As also there are not three incomprehensibles, nor three uncreated: but one incomprehensible, and one uncreated. So likewise the Father is Almighty, the Son Almighty: and the Holy Ghost Almighty. And yet there are not three Almighties: but one Almighty. So the Father is God, the Son is God: and the Holy Ghost is God. And yet there are not three Gods: but one God. So likewise the Father is Lord, the Son Lord: and the Holy Ghost Lord. And yet not three Lords: but one Lord. For like as we are compelled by the Christian truth to acknowledge every Person by himself to be God and Lord, so are we forbidden by the Catholic Religion to say, There be three Gods or three Lords. The Father is made of none: neither created nor begotten. The Son is of the Father alone: not made, nor created, but begotten. The Holy Ghost is of the Father and of the Son: neither made, nor created, nor begotten, but proceeding. So there is one Father, not three Fathers; one Son, not three Sons: one Holy Ghost, not three Holy Ghosts. And in this Trinity none is before or after another: none is greater or less than another: but the whole three Persons are coeternal together: and coequal. So that in all things, as is aforesaid: the Unity in Trinity, and the Trinity in Unity is to be worshiped. He, therefore, who will be saved must thus think of the Trinity.

"II. Furthermore, it is necessary to everlasting salvation: that he also believe rightly the incarnation of our Lord Jesus Christ. For the right Faith is, that we believe and confess: that our Lord Jesus Christ, the Son of God, is God and Man; God, of the Substance of the Father, begotten before the worlds: and Man, of the Substance of his Mother, born in the world: perfect God and perfect Man: of a reasonable soul and human flesh subsisting; equal to the Father, as touching his Godhead: and inferior to the Father, as touching his Manhood. Who, although he be God and Man, yet he is not two but one Christ; one, not by conversion of the Godhead into flesh, but by taking of the Manhood into God; one altogether; not by confusion of Substance: but by unity of Person. For as the reasonable soul and flesh is one Man, so God and Man is one Christ: who suffered for our salvation, descended into Hades,[4] rose again the third day from the dead. He ascended into heaven, he sitteth on the right hand of the Father, God Almighty: from whence he shall come to judge the quick and the dead. At whose coming all men shall rise again with their bodies: and shall give account for their own works. And they that have done good shall go into life everlasting: and they that have done evil into everlasting fire.

"This is the Catholic Faith: which except a man believe faithfully [*fideliter*] he cannot be saved.[5] Glory be to the Father, and to the Son: and to the Holy Ghost; as it was in the beginning, is now, and ever shall be: world without end. Amen."

The first sure mention of this document is found in the acts of a synod held at Autun [6] at the time when Saint Leodegar [7] was its bishop, that is, between the years 659 and 670. This council, or synod, passed several canons, or rules. The first canon stated that "if a cleric does not know exactly either the Apostolic Symbol or the Attestation of Faith of Saint Athanasius especially, let him be condemned by his bishop." The synod therefore exacted, under pain of episcopal condemnation, from every priest, deacon, subdeacon, or *clericus* assent to the Faith of Saint Athanasius — *Fides sancti Athanasii praesulis.* The context clearly shows that it was a question of the Quicunque vult, which is reproduced just above. After the Council of Autun the use of this Faith of Saint Athanasius spread more and more. A capitulary, that is, a regulation of Charlemagne, required that priests must learn the Catholic Faith of Saint Athanasius,[8] and about the year 800, Haito, bishop of Basel, exacted that the Faith of Saint Athanasius be learned by priests and be recited by heart every Sunday at the early morning service.[9]

The Faith of Saint Athanasius was hardly written by Athanasius himself, the great opponent of the Arians of whom we have spoken in a former chapter. As the second part of the Quicunque vult reflects the decisions of the Council of Chalcedon in 451, it must have been written long after Athanasius' death in 373. Further, this creed or symbol, which Calvin considered to be only a hymn, emerged among the Latin churches of the West. Its grammar shows that it must have been composed in Latin. Finally, against an Athanasian authorship is the fact that the Greek churches never recognized it or even knew it first.[10]

There is no evidence that this symbol or creed was used at baptism, or that it was to counteract a heresy or a particular philosophy, since at the time of its appearance the Western world in general and Gaul in particular were spiritual and intellectual deserts. The only purpose of this creed, therefore, must have been to teach the vital tenets of Christianity to the clergy.

After the Roman Empire disappeared in the West, the West became barbaric. Nothing was left of the military, political, juridical, and economic power of ancient Rome. Though everything was at its lowest ebb, one power remained. It was the Christian church. But even it was in danger of perishing in the stagnation of all things. To survive, it must engage in a counteroffensive and evangelize the countryside, which was still pagan. It must civilize the mores of the various Germanic tribes that had occupied the sundry places of the Western world and introduce the spirit of the Bible into the barbarians' customs.[11]

To achieve all this, the church needed a clergy well prepared for a counteroffensive against ignorance and sloth. But the clergy was not a force. A monk who wrote a history of the Merovingian kings of this time said sadly, "The world is growing old; keenness of intelligence is departing from us; there is no one in our days who pretends to compare with the orators of the past."[12] How could the clergy of this time draw inspiration from the Bible or the early church fathers when not only writing but even reading was a luxury unaccessible to clergymen and even to bishops?[13] What was needed, therefore, was a concise statement to be memorized that would sum up the essential truths to be accepted, thought, and taught about God and Jesus Christ. And this was the need that the Quicunque vult exactly met. It had a colossal success in the high Middle Ages. When it is read in the light of all its circumstances, many a reader will be tempted to call it the greatest intellectual and hence practical assertion of Christian faith ever made and written.

Let us examine first this symbol or creed more closely. Its general introduction sounds like a solemn law: Whosoever has the will to eternal salvation, and the certainty of it, must above all things hold fast to the Catholic Faith; for, if he does not keep it whole and inviolate, his eternal perdition is certain to follow.

This Catholic universal Faith consists, first of all, in worshiping one God " in Trinity, and the Trinity in Unity." This is a remarkable statement. Whereas the Apostolic and Nicene Creeds set forth first the Father, then the Son, and finally the Holy Ghost, and devoted an article to each of the three Persons in succession, the Quicunque vult sets forth the Trinity as a unit. There is only one true God. He is the Trinity as a whole. And the creed emphasizes this: The Godhead is altogether one: the Glory is coequal, the Majesty coeternal. The Father is eternal, the Son is eternal, and the Holy Spirit is eternal. And yet they are not three eternal, but one eternal. The author or authors of this creed were so insistent on this oneness of the Godhead that they placed the characters of each divine Person in balance through a series of synchronizations with the other two Persons so that the three would be conceived as a whole: " The Father is God, the Son is God: and the Holy Ghost is God. And yet there are not three Gods: but one God." This is a new note and a real contribution of this creed.

The final results of the Greek elaboration of the Trinity at the end of the fourth century may be formulated this way: three Persons or hypostases, which are the Father, the Son, and the Holy Spirit. These three Persons had previously been indifferently called *prosōpa* (aspects, faces, persons) or *hypostasis* (Latin, *substantia,* substance or subsisting subject, that is, person), but, in respect for the Nicene Council and in contrast to Sabellius, they came to be called in Greek *hypostaseis* only. As the Latin word corresponding to hypostasis was *essentia* (essence), the Latin preferred to speak of a Trinity of Persons (*personae*) in order not to be accused of believing in three divine essences. These three Persons or hypostases had one same divine *ousia* (substance or essence) in common by virtue of which they were one. But each Person or hypostasis had a particular propriety (Greek, *idiotēs*) in virtue of which each differed and was a distinct Person. The particular propriety of the Father was that he was not generated or begotten; the particularity of the Son was that he was generated or begotten; and the particular propriety of the Holy Spirit was that he proceeded or was sent. Such was the doctrine implicit in the dogmas of the Nicene and Chalcedonian statements. In contrast to them, the Quicunque vult sets forth one God—the Trinity. This notable advance was due to the influence of Augustine.

Augustine spoke of God in all his works, but he worked from about 399 to 416 on his book *De Trinitate*. And he brought this doctrine to perfection. While the Fathers before him had seen three Persons in one Substance, that is, taught a unity of species, Augustine conceived God as numerically one. In other words, the former fathers of the church had understood the prophets' statement, "There is but one God," as applying to the *Father*. Augustine understood that sentence as applying to the *Trinity*. There is but one God—the Trinity. God is numerically one. There is only the Trinity God. As for the Persons of the Father, the Son, and Holy Spirit, these are different relationships into which the Absolute Spirit enters with itself. God, of course, is beyond man's understanding, but Augustine sought to express the incomprehensible through similes taken from familiar facts. Just as man is one and yet has memory, intellect, and will,[14] so God is one, yet in him are processes: the Father is God's thought thinking of self, and that corresponds to our memory; the Son is the objective thought of God,[15] and that corresponds to our intellect; the

Holy Spirit is God's awareness that the subject (Father) and the object (Son) of his thought are one, or the will to bind them together.[16] Thus for Augustine the three Persons are not members but inner relationships of the Trinity God.

Augustine did not mean to be dogmatic and definitive about all this, because, he says, " we may sooner exhaust the ocean with a shell than this subject with human language." Then he himself said that " he spoke of all this not in order really to say something but in order not to remain silent."[17] Striving to express the inexpressible, Augustine also used the order of nature to illustrate his insight. Just as nature has a general being, particular existences, and a general order (*esse, species et ordo*), so does God.[18] The *De Trinitate* also states that the union of the three terms of the Trinity is such that each term encloses the other two, and the total of the three is equal to any one of the three.[19] In his last work, *The City of God,* Augustine summed up his teaching about the Trinity as follows: " We faithfully [*fideliter*] believe, maintain, and preach that the Father has begotten the Word, that is, Wisdom through whom all things were made, his only Son, like him one, like him eternal, like him supremely good; that the Holy Spirit is altogether the Spirit of the Father and the Son, consubstantial and coeternal with the Father and the Son; because of the propriety of persons, a Trinity, because of inseparable divinity, one God only; and because of inseparable omnipotence, almighty; and all together they are not three Gods or three Almighties; so inseparable the Unity of the three Persons is, that by himself he willed that it be so preached."[20]

This teaching of Augustine is exactly the teaching of the first part of the Quicunque vult: the Catholic universal Faith consists in believing in one God in Trinity and a Trinity in one God, neither confusing the Persons[21] nor separating the Substance.[22] In this Trinity none is before or after another; none is greater or lesser than another, but the whole three Persons are altogether eternal and perfectly equal, so that in all things, as is aforesaid, we must worship the Unity in Trinity and the Trinity in Unity. The contribution of the Quicunque vult was not in stopping ancient heresies that no longer endangered the church but in exhibiting the Trinity in sharp focus.

The second part of the Quicunque vult is about the incarnation of Jesus Christ. It is not enough for him who desires to be saved to believe and to worship the Trinity. It is absolutely necessary to his eternal salvation that he also believe faithfully (*fideliter*) the incarnation of our Lord Jesus Christ. For, as Augustine repeatedly said, "He was the partaker in our mortality, that we mortal men may be participant of his divinity."[23] In the Quicunque vult we find a new element about the Person of Christ which makes this a doubly superior creed.

For many years great debates about the Person of Christ had been going on in the Eastern churches because some teachers there were insisting on a radical distinction between the divine and human natures in Christ. For them the human nature in Jesus Christ had to remain inviolate, intact, and whole because if the human nature of Christ had not been real, he would not have truly suffered, died, and risen. In a word, unless fully man, Christ would not have lifted mankind up to God, and hence Christ would not be our Deliverer and Savior.

The Council of Chalcedon in 451 finally accepted a formula known as "The Tome of Leo" because it was sponsored by the delegates of Pope Leo the Great: "We confess one and same Jesus Christ, only Son of God, whom we acknowledge to be in two natures without confusion,[24] without change,[25] without division,[26] without separation."[27] These words were rather negative. They condemned, indeed, the Monophysites and Nestorians, but suggested no further step. It is not enough to condemn the wrong ways. One must indicate the right way. And this is what the Quicunque vult does. It is still the best attempt to translate in rational, or at least clear, terms the paradox of two natures, the divine and the human, united [28] and perfectly balanced in Christ:

"For the right Faith is that we believe and confess that our Lord Jesus Christ, the Son of God, is God and Man. . . . Perfect God and perfect Man . . . One altogether; not by confusion of Substance: but by unity of Person . . . although he be God and Man; yet he is not two but one Christ; One, not by conversion of the Divinity into human flesh, but inasmuch as God has taken humanity to himself. Christ is One not by confusion of natures but by the unity of the Person."

All this may be unbelievable to some, yet the Quicunque vult not only asserts that "this is the Catholic Faith: which except a man believe faithfully [*fideliter*] he cannot be saved," but this creed concludes its presentation of the Trinity and the incarnation as the quintessence of Christianity, with this warning of a last judgment:

"God and Man in one Christ . . . suffered for our salvation: descended into the Abode of the Dead, rose again the third day from the dead. He ascended into heaven and now sitteth on the right hand of . . . God Almighty but from there he shall come to judge the living and the dead. At his coming all men shall rise again with their bodies: and shall give account of their works. And they who have done good shall go into life everlasting; and they who have done evil into everlasting fire."

As for the writer of the Quicunque vult, we shall probably never know who he was. Among modern scholars, Brewer attributed the creed to Ambrose; Kattenbusch and Burn assigned it to a monk in Southern Gaul; Künstle gave it to some Spanish theologian; Morin and Turmel attributed it to Caesarius of Arles; Stiglmayr to Fulgentius of Ruspe; Waterland assigned it to Hilary of Poitiers (d. 367); Muratori gave it to Venantius Fortunatus, bishop of Poitiers in the sixth century. A conjecture traces it to Virgilius of Thapsus, an African bishop who composed a treatise on the Trinity in the fifth century. Others finally attributed it to Vincent of Lérins. Vincent was a monk living in Southeastern Gaul who wrote a marvelous book called the *Commonitorium* in 434. As a booklet of sentences of Vincent of Lérins (*Excerpta Vincentii Lirinensis*), discovered and published by J. Madoz in 1940, contains statements characteristic of the Quicunque vult, we may conclude that if Vincent did not write the Quicunque vult himself, it was written according to the works and spirit of Vincent of Lérins sometime between 434 and 670 somewhere in Gaul, which today is called France.[29]

V

THE ROLE OF THE CREEDS IN THE HIGH MEDIEVAL CHURCH

When the church was definitively organized, it was shaped on the model of the Roman Empire.[1] As Rome declined, much of its glory and power passed into the church and still lives therein. A man who unwillingly engineered or helped this historical phenomenon was Ambrose. Originally, he was a Roman official with an excellent education. As the Christians in Milan were quarreling over whom to elect bishop, Ambrose had to come to quell the rioters. It occurred to them to elect Ambrose as their bishop. He accepted and brought into the Christian church all the thought, dignity, poise, and governing ability of a high Roman official. By adapting Cicero's treatise *On Duties* to the Christian clergy, Ambrose by his own book, *On Duties of the Clergy,* also further Stoicized the Christian outlook on life and ethics. The extent of Bishop Ambrose's authority is seen in his ability to humiliate an emperor by causing him to repent and do penance.

Ancient Christians already preferred to settle matters in church rather than in court, but now with the Empire declining, the Emperor Valentinian made the bishops defenders and protectors of cities. Bishops became magistrates, inheriting the pagan position of the city-priest (flamen). Like him, the bishop now sat in the court (*curia*), handling public projects and all sorts of local matters. All cases of conscience, marriage, separation, and wills came to be referred to the bishop. He soon became the first civic magistrate of the city as well as its spiritual shepherd. As the Roman state got weaker, the church became stronger and stronger. It became a real state with all the organs essential to a government.[2] What mattered most to the Western bishops and the clergy, who had come to these positions of responsibility, was not the adherence of everyone to an infinity of small tenets of theology but rather the unity of the Christian churches. When Cyprian and Augustine had said that " outside the church there is no salvation," they meant, not doctrines, not fussy little details about Scripture interpretation, but rather the discipline and loyalty to the church.[3]

The man who laid a rational foundation for the unity of Christians in the fifth century was Vincent of Lérins. " To be a Catholic," he wrote, " is to hold what has been believed always, everywhere, and by all."[4] Vincent of Lérins did not have in mind that infinity of minute and precise doctrines which certain modern sects have invented and now demand from all men. The reason is that in the fifth century the many tenets of certain modern sects did not exist. What did Vincent mean, then, by " Faith? " In his mind, the " Catholic Faith " was what held together the Christians who lived in Gaul, around the Mediterranean basin, with the possible addition of Britain. And what held them together was what the Latins called *fides,* that is, faithfulness. The *Catholica Fides* was the faithfulness or allegiance of Christians, their devotion to one system of ecclesiastical discipline. It was not so much the correctness of their views as their fidelity that made them members of the Catholic Church. For Augustine and Vincent of Lérins, the body of the " faithful " — the *fideles* — were those who were trustworthy in a single allegiance.[5] The faith which was established in the Western world was a rule of allegiance rather than a statement of truths or beliefs in the modern sense.

The principle of ancient Roman unity, of course, was the axiom that the whole social fabric, public and private morality, ultimately depended upon religion. But by the word religion, the ancient Romans meant awe, reverence, and conscientiousness in the performance of all the duties relating to the worship of the gods.[6] What we moderns call inward or personal religion, the Romans called *pietas* (piety). Our modern society is held together by economy and calculated interest. The early Roman community was held together by an emotive element called *pietas*. For Cicero, this *pietas* meant dutiful respect toward the gods, the fatherland, parents, and kinsmen.[7] Cicero added that piety was simple equity. " Equity itself," he said, " is divided into three parts: one part is devoted to the gods above; another to the spirits of the dead below; and a third to men. The first is called piety; the second sanctity; the third justice or equity." [8] It is hard for us moderns to understand how piety or personal religion can be " justice or equity " toward God.[9] But for Cicero himself this matter was simple. " The gods," he wrote, " are of so glorious and excellent a nature that a wise man is induced by their excellence to worship them." [10] " The gods," he continues, " are not only lords and moderators of all things but likewise great benefactors of men; hence, men should observe the laws out of gratitude toward the gods." [11] Hence, piety is gratefully giving back to God what belongs to him.[12] And what is this but justice and equity?

The ancient Romans believed that consecrated formulas and gestures had a magical effect. In the oldest Roman law it was not enough to present the case in court; one had to go through a symbolic process, use certain words, and make certain gestures. Before the court each case was a pantomime: to protest against a neighbor who had erected a wall, a stone was thrown against the wall. The Romans thus came to understand well only what they could see. The physical gestures acted out in court served to represent to them that justice which cannot be seen. Further, the

Romans were formalists; that is, they scrupulously respected their ancient formulas. In justice they obeyed the letter of the law, without caring for its meaning. For them, every formula was sacred and ought to be strictly applied. In cases before the court, their maxim was: "Let the law be what the tongue has already pronounced." If a party, therefore, made a mistake in one word in reciting the formula in court, his case was lost. A man entered a case against his neighbor for having cut down his vines: the traditional formula that he had to use in court contained the word "tree" (*arbor*), not "vine" (*vinea*). If he, however, said the word "vine" (which in this particular case was the right word), he would lose his case. The administration of justice, therefore, was a sort of ritual.[13]

What he believed or how he felt was, with the ancient Roman, a matter of small concern compared with the way he worshiped. It was not the spirit that counted but the ceremony itself that the Roman thought to have power with the gods. The Roman covered his ears when engaged in prayer. When offering sacrifice, he covered his whole head with his robe so as to be sure that no word of evil omen or no sight of an evil eye could possibly reach him. The Latin word for "adoration" means "bringing to the mouth." The Roman expressed his adoration by raising his right hand to the mouth and kissing it,[14] but the one essential thing in prayer was the correct repetition, in a clear and distinct voice, of the prescribed formulas as they were preserved from ancient times. The change of a single syllable, the omission or wrong pronunciation of a single word, was a dishonor to the deity and rendered the entire service worse than worthless. This rigid adherence to ancient and traditional forms, which was characteristic of the Romans, is important in our history. It was one of the legacies that the Romans left to their Christian successors. Another legacy was the value attached to frequent repetitions of the same prayer.[15]

All this has a bearing on the function of our creeds, as we shall soon realize.

In the ancient Latin-speaking churches, the creed was an expression of confidence and reliance. And that creed was part of a ritual. These Christians were Romans. Now they followed the new Christian rites even more meticulously than they had adhered to Roman rituals. Doctrine and fervor mattered little in the religion of the ancient Romans. What mattered was the ritual. The Romans conceived all the aspects of their daily life to be subject to the power of external forces (called " numina "), which animated nature and which the Romans were anxious to have on their side.[16] Their priests and colleges of priests existed for no other reason than to perform these rituals exactly, so as to please the gods and keep them on their side. The Romans wanted their gods to be their business associates in order that the business would be profitable. In this respect, the ancient Romans foreshadowed something of certain contemporary teachings that consider God as an instrument of men's success. Cicero was nobler when he said that " if we cast off piety toward the gods, faithfulness [*fides*] and all the associations of human life, and that most excellent of virtues called justice, may perish." [17]

For better or for worse, the church in the West inherited this Roman formalism, literalism, and utilitarianism. And like the Romans, the Western churchmen, from the fifth to the ninth century, firmly believed that the unity of the church depended upon the ritual. The recitation in Latin of the Apostolic, Nicene, and Quicunque vult Creeds was a part of the Catholic ritual. And in the Roman tradition, it was the very essence of a ritual that the formulas recited should always, everywhere, and by all means be the same. The intellectual meaning of the creed mattered little in those days; what mattered was the role and the efficacy of the formula. The creeds and the liturgy were recited in Latin.

taking the place of the worship of ancient gods. Pagan festivals were transformed into Christian holy days. The Feast of All Saints took the place of the pagan Judgment of the Dead, and the Purification of the Virgin Mary occupied the place of the *februa,* which once purified the people and honored the dead.[21] The dead, however, were not abandoned to their lot. The church took them in and made them participant in our redemption. The church is not confined to Gaul; it encompasses heaven and earth and a large purgatory in between. But the bishops never lost sight of earth. The Council of Narbonne in 589 ordered those lazy men who still observed the Day of Jupiter (Thursday) to forget Jupiter and go to work on that day.

As we may see, the ancient Western church was now concerned not with heresies but with conduct. The unconscious fear of the church leaders was that the barbarians, who once destroyed the unity of the Roman Empire, might now divide the church. Hence, the bishops resurrected a custom of the druids — pagan priests who knew how to keep the Gauls in line. Caesar, some fifty years before Christ, narrated that " if a private or public man refused to subscribe to the sentence of the druids, they would bar him from sacrifices, and this, for the Gauls, was the greatest penalty. Those who were struck by it were put in the rank of outlaws and godless men. Everybody would avoid meeting them and talking to them for fear that any contact with them would be fatal. No legal action was open to them, and they were excluded from all men." [22] Excommunication, which had for centuries pre-existed in Gaul, thus became a fearful weapon in the hands of the Christian clergy. But it preserved unity.

Under Charlemagne (742–814), bishops finally entered the central government. At a great annual assembly held at the court for state business, bishops and abbots deliberated with counts and warriors, and being ordinarily better educated, they wrote the laws. The great idea of Charlemagne was that all Christian peoples formed one community, one grand commonwealth. Under him the Christian nations were one family with one emperor and with one pope at the head.

Pope and emperor, church and state — but which of these two came first? Which one should appoint the bishops? Some three hundred years after Charlemagne, this rivalry of papacy and empire came to a head. This time the strong man in the West turned out to be the pope. The prestige of the city of Rome, visited by Peter and Paul, stores of ancient customs and new legends, energetic personalities, and the luck of circumstances had made the papacy. Since the Arabs, for example, had occupied most of the East and Africa, the pope no longer had any competitor there. The West now looked to the pope as the bishop of all bishops and the representative of Christ on earth. Led by such great men as Gregory VII (1020–1085) and Innocent III (1198–1216), the papacy reached the summit of power.

But summit implies a decline. First England, then France, had consolidated into sturdy kingdoms. There the spirit of nationality or patriotism undermined that sense of human and divine unity which was the glory of the high Middle Ages when men in Europe felt that they were one great community under one God, one emperor, and one pope. The church then became wealthy, and people now complained about the riches and luxury of the clergy. Worst of all, when the medieval church had reached its zenith, the papacy and Christendom ventured into some eight Crusades — the first in 1096, the last in 1270. Their object was to reconquer the tomb of Jesus and the Holy Land of Palestine, which had fallen into Mohammedan hands.

The crusaders started off, self-confident, even conceited, about their religion and ways, and proud of their weapons and physical strength. But on seeing the infidels close at hand, the crusaders found most of them to be grave, enlightened, honest, reliable, generous (for example, Saladin, who sent his own physician to care for a crusader chief who was sick), and they began to respect them. This contact with the East and Arabic civilization or culture greatly changed the ideas and ways of medieval Christians. The crusaders, who were hardly able to count, found that the Arabs knew algebra, trigonometry, and some chemistry. To the Arabs of Spain and Sicily, Europeans owe a rebirth of medicine, surgery, poetry, philosophy, and the development of several manufactures and devices, such as gunpowder and paper and the mariner's compass.[23]

The real force in history is not money but culture, that is, a certain refinement of the intellect and sentiment. Medieval Christendom wanted to conquer the East but fell a victim to a superior Arabic culture. The Crusades mark the decline of the medieval church and the beginning of all sorts of currents and undercurrents which led to such a fragmentation of medieval unity that it passed out, not with a bang, but with a whimper.

VI

THE WALDENSIAN DECLARATIONS OF FAITH

THE LAST CHAPTER ended with an allusion to the breaking up of medieval unity. Such a unity was a reality in the sense that in the high Middle Ages the peoples of Europe felt themselves to be one great Christian community under one pope and one emperor. The evidence for this is the fact that the creation of modern national states and various nationalisms was unable to suppress altogether the common awareness that Europe was once, and may again be, one great Christian community as it was, let us say, under Charlemagne. When we speak of medieval unity, however, we do not ignore the fact that in that unity there existed a great variety of opinions and philosophical currents, and that the absolute jurisdiction and unity of the Catholic Church had serious opponents. The most famous competitors of medieval Catholicism were the Cathari and the Waldensians.

The Cathari, properly speaking, were not heretics but a religious group altogether different from Christianity, which had come into Europe from the Balkans. The foundation of the Catharite doctrine was the perpetual problem of evil. The Cathari accounted for the presence of sufferings and injustices in this world by saying that since the beginning there were and are two principles: good and evil. From the good principle came Light and Spirit; from the evil principle came darkness and matter. Hence, the Cathari abstained from the world of matter as far as possible.

The Cathari were not envious of the wealth of the Catholic clergy, were not men in revolt or dissidents, but were men with convictions, who often preferred to perish in fire rather than to give up their beliefs. Such complete faith could spring only from within. The Cathari did not (as some old records have it) practice suicide. The truth is that as the church could not possibly admit any martyrdom among the Cathari, their martyrs were misrepresented as suicides. Nor is it true that the Cathari were sexually promiscuous. This was simply a rumor arising out of the fact that the Cathari did not marry in the Catholic Church but in communities of their own. Nor were they antisocial, for they gained the respect of the lords and the populations of Southern France and became so numerous there that it took a great crusade of pope and king to crush them. One million perished, and their religion is utterly extinct.[1]

The Waldensians were an altogether different movement. Until recently their origins were debated and obscure, even to the Waldensians themselves. So, for example, at the time of the French Revolution, the Waldensian official explanation was that their church went back to the time of Claude, bishop of Turin. It was he who opposed the worship of images and said that we should carry the cross rather than worship it. When Napoleon Bonaparte descended into Northwestern Italy in 1805 and received at Turin a deputation of the Waldensians, this is the conversation which reportedly took place between them:

"Are you one of the Protestant clergy of this country?" said Bonaparte to Peyran, who was the speaker of the deputation.

"Yes, sire, I am the moderator of the Waldensian Church."

"Are you schismatics from the Church of Rome?" asked the Emperor.

"Not schismatics, I hope, but separate for reason of conscience, and this we Waldensians believe to be according to the Scriptures," answered the moderator.

"You have had brave men among you . . . but your mountains are yet the best defenders you can have. Caesar with his five legions had difficulty in passing through your defiles. . . ."

"Yes, sire; but we believe that our people were helped by divine Providence."

"How long have you formed an independent church?"

"From the days of Claude, bishop of Turin, about the year 820."

"What stipend does your clergy receive?"

"We have no fixed stipend. . . ."

"Are you organized?"[2]

"No, sire."

"Prepare a memorandum; send it to Paris, and you will immediately obtain the organization and a monthly check."

According to recent research, the Waldensians did not originate at the time of Claude, nor were they an uninterrupted continuation of the apostolic church, nor a combination of anterior movements. Waldism was started by Valdes, a rich merchant in Lyons, France. The Waldensians were so called after this man whom English-speaking peoples know as Waldo. One day he was impressed by a minstrel who was singing in a square the "Story of Saint Alexis." This is one of the most ancient poems of French literature, written before the year 1050. It told the story of a rich young man in the city of Rome who, abhorring marriage, ran away from his father's house. He went into the East, took the vow of poverty, and spent his life as a beggar in Laodicea and Edessa. Returning home, he asked his parents for alms so that they might pile up a treasure in heaven. All he got from them was a miserable dwelling under their stairway. Only after his death was he recognized by some sign hidden under his miserable and ragged clothes. He was lucky to receive at least a burial. This story means little to practical men of today but in those days it was a moving story and greatly impressed Waldo. He took the minstrel into his house so as to understand better the verses that extolled ancient faith and by contrast debased the riches and wealth of men. Next day, brooding about the frailty of life and the vanity of the world, Waldo went to consult a master of theology, asking him, " Which is the surest and perfect way to God? " The answer was Jesus' words to the rich young man, " If you wish to be perfect, sell all your goods and give them to the poor " (Matt. 19:21).

Waldo decided to obey the order of Jesus. Returning home, he assured a life income to his wife, placed his two daughters in an abbey in Poitou, and during a great famine (which we may identify with that of 1176), gave most of his fortune to the poor. Moreover, he hired two priests to translate and make copies of large portions of the Bible in the current language of the people. This " conversion " of Waldo was a sensation in the city of Lyons. A crowd gathered around his place, and Waldo preached to them:

" Friends and Citizens! You cannot serve two incompatible lords such as God and mammon! I am not out of my mind as you think. I simply got even with an enemy which tyrannized me: money! which occupied a larger place in my heart than God did, so that I served the creature instead of the Creator. Whatever I publicly do, I do for my sake and for your sake: for my sake, because if you still find me having money, I wish you to say that I am out of my mind; for your sake, because I wish you to put your hope in God rather than in goods which perish."

As these views of Waldo's did not correspond exactly with those of the community, he was criticized by the many, yet approved by some. These gathered in a group around Waldo and practiced " evangelical poverty," that is, simplicity as found in the Gospels. But Waldo knew that the disciples of Jesus also preached, hence he must preach and send off his followers, two by two, as the Gospels say (Matt. 10:5; Luke 10:1). The local bishop Guichard, however, not understanding the perfect purity of Waldo's intentions, did not grant his companions permission to circulate in Lyons. Hence, Waldo went to see Pope Alexander III to get authority to preach. The pope welcomed Waldo affably but referred this matter to the Third Lateran Council. Walter Map, an English priest, was attending this assembly in Rome at this time (1179). In a curious satirical work entitled "On the Trifles of Courtiers" (*Liber de nugis curialium*) he narrates how he was invited by a bishop in the Council to question Waldo and his companion about Christian doctrine.

"Do you believe in God the Father?" asked Map.
"We believe," answered the Waldensians.
"Do you believe in the Son?"
"We do."
"Do you believe in the Holy Spirit?"
"We do."
"And in the mother of Christ?"

As the Waldensians answered, "We believe," to this question, "the whole assembly burst into laughter and all mocked them," narrates Map. The reason for this hilarity was that Catholics use the words "believe in" only with reference to the Persons of the Trinity and never with reference to creatures. The last answer was taken as a proof of the theological ignorance of the Waldensians; hence the pope forbade them to preach.

With their main vocation and function denied to them, "the Poor Men of Lyons," or Waldensians, had to face this dilemma: either obey and thus disappear or disobey and exclude themselves from the church. The simple Waldo, being a sincere Catholic and wanting to serve the church, never dreamed that he would have to face such an alternative. But Walter Map had a keener insight into the real situation and an understanding of clerical organizations. "The Waldensians have no fixed residence," writes Map. "They lead an itinerant life; they walk two by two, without shoes and with a woolen tunic. They do not own anything of their own but, like the apostles, hold all things in common; naked, they follow a naked Christ. They could not begin more humbly but they should not be allowed to enter [and take part in the activity of the church] because, should we let them in, they would displace and chase us out." [3]

Waldo found, indeed, that he had to live the words "We must obey God rather than men" (Acts 5:29). He and his people decided to persist in their inner calling to preach, and thereby excluded themselves from the church. They were, indeed, soon excommunicated by John Bellesmains, bishop of Lyons, and censured by Pope Lucius III at the Synod of Verona, 1184. Expelled from Lyons, the Waldensian brethren and sisters had to scatter and live in hiding. Their scattering resulted in the spreading of their teaching. However, they received reinforcement in the sense that many Humiliates in Italy came to recognize the authority of Waldo. The Humiliates were a group of penitents in Lombardy. Some of them were priests, others, monks; the majority were laymen, but they all strove to live by the monastic rule of Saint Benedict. The Waldensian movement, thus strengthened, soon spread in the large cities of France, Italy, Germany, Austria, Bohemia (where Waldo died sometime between 1197 and 1217), and even Spain. There, in 1194, King Alphonso II made a law confiscating all possessions of "the *Insabatati* [wearers of wooden shoes], called also Waldensians or Poor Men of Lyons." In 1197, King Pedro II added then penalty of fire, and in 1211 some eighty Waldensians were burned at the stake.

A Profession of Faith (*Professio fidei*) signed by Waldo between the years 1181 and 1184 was found a few years ago. Therein, taking an oath in his own name and in the name of his companions, Waldo adheres to the Christian dogmas and professes the following articles of faith: unity of nature and Trinity of Persons in God; God creator and orderer of all things, visible and invisible; author of two covenants and of the mission of John the Baptist; Jesus Christ as truly God and truly man; one only holy, apostolic, and spotless Catholic Church outside of which there is no salvation; efficacy of sacraments within the church even when performed by a sinner; infant baptism and its regenerating value or efficacy; confirmation by the hands of bishops; the real presence of Christ in the Eucharist; necessity of both repentance and satisfactory deeds in order to obtain from God remission of sins; extreme unction; condemnation of divorce and permission to widowed persons to remarry; validity of all the orders of the church hierarchy; permission to eat meat; resurrection of the flesh; the Last Judgment; prayer for the dead. Waldo's creed ends by a profession of voluntary poverty.

At the beginning of his apostolate, therefore, Waldo was an orthodox and loyal Catholic. Opposed by the local clergy, he had appealed to the pope, whom he recognized as the head of the church and the voucher of both orthodoxy and purity of morals. Abandoned by the pope, Waldo had to rely more and more on the Scriptures, even disregarding church ordinances. In his time, Waldo was thus the initiator of a new type of preaching based not on church ethics but on a purely personal knowledge of the Bible which, as we saw, Waldo sought to bring to even the lowest classes and in their own current idioms. This Biblicism gave a unique character to the Waldensian movement and made it, among the various heretical and spiritual medieval movements, the only one to have a clear Christian orientation in spite of divisions and hesitations that were to last until Reformation times.

For Waldo, the Word of God was not only the source of faith and ethics but also of social organization. Waldo created fervent communities modeled after the pattern of the early apostolic groups described in the New Testament. Their ideals may be found in an ancient Waldensian "Book Against Heresy" (*Liber antiheresis*), which has been recently found. As a whole this work was directed against the Cathari, yet here and there it criticizes the corruption, if not of the head, certainly of the members, of the

Catholic Church. The book expresses the desire of the Waldensians to be relieved of all manual labor so as to consecrate their bodies and souls to meditation, prayer, and preaching to all men. The Waldensian writers claim this privilege on the basis of its being a grace received directly from God. It is a call, they say, from neither pope nor archbishops, but from God himself. It is God, they write, who authorizes and even urges them to this ministry.[4]

The basic idea of Waldo was a return to the apostolic way of life and preaching. The fundamental principle of the Waldensians was the authority of the Bible, which they took to the letter. They knew large portions of it by heart. In their meetings they read parts of the Scripture, explained them and prayed. They believed that "lies kill the soul." They disapproved of oaths, the death penalty, and revenge. They did not admit the existence of purgatory on the ground that there are only two ways or roads: one leading to life and the other to death.

After the time of Waldo there were two currents of Waldism. Waldensians in France were moderate, whereas those in Italy were extremists. The latter went so far as to say that the Roman Church was of the devil, that prelates were nothing but Pharisees, that the laity were not inferior to the priest and in the true church all are equal, that a devout layman is more truly a priest and can give the Communion better than those who govern the church. The strength of the Waldensians lay in the fact that they led a poor and simple life in contrast to the manners of a too rich and often corrupt clergy, and that their preachers addressed the people in their own tongue.

To whatever extent the Waldensians may eventually have diverged from the Catholic Church, originally they were good Catholics. Excommunicated and expelled at the outset, they were schismatics rather than heretics. Their extant ancient prose writings quote from Augustine, Bernard, Isidore, and Thomas Aquinas; and their ancient poem, called "The Bark," was simply a popular adaptation of Pope Innocent III's book "On the Contempt of the World." Most famous of the Waldensian poems is the "Noble Lesson," which consists of 479 Alexandrine verses. It is a noble lesson, that is, a summary of sacred history with an edifying warning drawn from the Bible. Its composition probably goes back to the thirteenth century. It is written in Romanic, a language that was no longer Latin and not yet French but something in between. The "Noble Lesson" opens with the assertion that the world is near its end. Humanity has successively rejected three God-given laws: natural law, Moses' law, and Christ's law. Hence, leaving aside gold and silver, we must keep watch, for the Final Judgment is imminent, and pray that we may be of the number of God's elect to dwell in his court forever.[5]

A student of ancient Waldensian literature, H. J. Chaytor, rightly observes that Waldensian invectives against the luxury and venality of the clergy were mild in comparison to the verses of contemporary Catholic troubadours on the same subject. It is to the credit of the Waldensians, he says, that they appeared to be more anxious to improve the morality of their own members than to criticize the shortcomings of the Catholic Church. Much stress was laid upon asceticism of life and the evils of the flesh in terms that almost coincide with dualism. Exhortations to avoid the temptations of the world and to practice prayer, fasting, and works of charity were reinforced by contrasting the life of sinners with those of the good, and by lurid allusions to the horrors of hell. In the background of these admonitions the prevalent idea was that the Day of Judgment was at hand, an idea that we have already seen in the opening and closing lines of the "Noble Lesson."[6]

With these simple beliefs, the Waldensians brought upon themselves all sorts of inquisitions, persecutions, deportations, and massacres throughout the Middle Ages, misfortunes that the

Waldensians patiently endured as the lot of true believers. The medieval church had indeed become a theocratic monarchy with lordship over peoples and kings: it claimed to be the true and infallible church out of which there was neither salvation nor truth. For centuries the Waldensians withstood such a claim on the basis of the Scriptures. In spite of persecutions and massacres, they survived to the Reformation. And when the echo of Luther's mighty voice in 1517 against abuses and the news of Zwingli's practical reforms in Zurich reached the Waldensians, they received new life. Historians assert that they rejoiced that Luther and his fellow Reformers had enthroned the principle of the Scripture as the Word of God in a large part of Christendom. The reports that many were leaving the papacy and turning to the gospel as the source of truth gave a new hope to their cause.

Thus many Waldensians became vitally interested in the events beyond the Alps. Already in 1526 the Waldensians of Italy had sent two of their ministers (whom they called *Barba*), Martin Gonin, of the Valley of Lucerne, and Guy of Calabria, to Switzerland and Germany to observe what went on there and to report back to the churches of Italy. Four years later the Waldensians of Provence and Dauphiné sent two deputies, George Morel of Perindol and Peter Masson of Burgundy, to the Reformers of Switzerland and Germany. They first met Farel in Neuchâtel, then Haller in Bern, Oecolampadius in Basel and finally Bucer in Strassburg. On his return, Peter Masson was arrested and put to death as an Evangelical. But Morel escaped detection and returned safely to Provence. There the Basel Reformer, Oecolampadius, had sent this letter of encouragement to him to stand up boldly:

"You know that with the heart one believes unto righteousness and with the mouth one makes profession unto salvation, but those who are ashamed of Christ in this world will not be acknowledged by him before his Father. As our God is a God of truth, he wants to be served in reality. As God is a jealous God, he does not permit his own to put themselves under the yoke of the antichrist. No agreement is possible between Christ and Belial. . . . Those who know themselves to have been redeemed by the blood of Christ must be courageous. Better to be dead than conquered." [7]

The Waldensians thus became related to the Reformation, and the Reformers Bucer and Oecolampadius "certainly acknowledged that Christ was in the Waldensians, and they loved them as brethren." [8] As noted above, since the time of Waldo there had been two branches of Waldensians. Those of Lombardy, or Italy, in spite of Waldo's opposition, denied the validity of the sacraments administered by Catholic priests; they ordained their own ministers and had an order of worship of their own. The Waldensians of Provence, Dauphiné, and Languedoc, or France, on the other hand, had kept some contact with the Catholic Church and frequented the mass. Bucer and Oecolampadius recognized that the Waldensians of France had, in spite of the thick surrounding darkness, kept the knowledge and love of truth, yet the two Reformers wanted these brethren to cease attending the mass and to cut all connections with the Catholic Church.

As the Reformers' ideas became known among the Waldensians, the question arose whether or not they should adhere to the Reformation. A general convention was summoned at Cianforan, a small village in the Italian Alps, on September 12, 1532. All Waldensian ministers and so many faithful were present that the convention had to take place in the open air and under the shadow of magnificent chestnut trees. Three Reformed delegates came from beyond the Alps: Antony Saunier, originally from Dauphiné, Pierre Robert Olivétan of Noyon, a friend or relative of Calvin, and Guillaume Farel. For six days the principles of the Reformation were debated. The long and lively discussion was led and dominated by Farel. He decisively influenced the majority of the Waldensians to accept the propositions of the Reformers,[9] which then and there were formulated into the following Declaration of Faith:

"*We believe that*

"1. Worship must be performed in spirit and in truth because God is Spirit and wills that those who worship him worship him in Spirit and in truth;

"2. All those who have been and shall be saved have been elected of God before the foundation of the world;

"3. It is impossible that those who have been ordained to salvation should not be saved;

"4. Whosoever believes in man's free will wholly denies God's predestination and grace;

"5. There is no good deed except that which God has prescribed, and no bad deed except that which God has forbidden;

"6. A Christian may take an oath in the name of God without going against that which is written in chapter 5 of Saint Matthew (verse 34), provided that he who takes the oath does not take the name of the Lord in vain. Now it is not in vain when the oath is directed to the glory of God and to the salvation of a man's neighbor. Moreover, it is permissible to take an oath before a magistrate because he who has that office (whether he is a believer or an unbeliever) holds his authority from God;

"7. Auricular confession is not commanded by God nor determined by the Holy Scripture; the Christian's true confession is to confess only to God to whom honor and glory belong. There is another kind of confession, when one becomes reconciled to his neighbor, of which Matthew 5:23-25 (and James 5:16) speak; a third kind of confession is when one, having committed some public offense, does also publicly confess his fault;

"8. On Sunday we should cease from our earthly works out of zeal for God, out of love for our servants,[10] and in order to apply ourselves to the hearing of the Word of God;

"9. It is not permissible for a Christian to take revenge upon his enemy in any way whatsoever;

"10. A Christian may exercise the office of a magistrate over other Christians;[11]

"11. There is no determination of time for any Christian fast, and it cannot be found in the Scripture that God has commanded and appointed any special days;

"12. Marriage is not prohibited to any one of whatever condition he be;

"13. Those who forbid matrimony teach a diabolical doctrine;

"14. Whosoever has not the gift of continence should contract matrimony;

"15. The ministers of the Word of God must not be transferred from one place to another except it be for some great good to the church;

"16. Ministers' possessing some private goods in order to feed their family is not incompatible with apostolic communion;

"17. Concerning sacraments, the Scripture shows that Christ left only two, namely, Baptism and the Eucharist, or Holy Supper, which we receive in order to show that we persevere in the holy faith according to our baptismal obligation, and in order to celebrate the memory of the Passion of Jesus Christ who is our redemption and has washed us of our sins by his precious blood."[12]

The Waldensians were thus led to enter the wider world of Protestantism and become a part of the Reformation. It is now time that we turn our attention to the Protestant Reformation and find out what its original faith really was.

VII

THE LUTHERAN CONFESSION OF AUGSBURG, 1530

THE PROTESTANT REFORMATION was such a vast and complex movement that it cannot be easily defined. According to some Catholic historians, its main cause was the concupiscence of Luther and other monks who wished to be free from the church and its discipline. Other historians, however, maintain that, unless European women in those days were far more beautiful than they are today, it is just impossible that the lust of a few monks could have produced such a catastrophe as the collapse of the Catholic Church in half of Europe. Hence, other Catholic authors prefer to attribute the Reformation to political greed. Germany was a loose confederation of several states under a nominal emperor. Many princes and city mayors were anxious to obtain the great wealth of the church of Jesus Christ so as to remedy their financial plight. Protestant historians, on the other hand, call attention to the moral conditions of the time. The corruption of the clergy and the greed of the papacy would have caused this vast revolt against Roman domination. Others, such as Max Weber, emphasize the economic causes of the Protestant Reformation, which seem to them to have been the theological expression of an upset European economy. Personally I cannot help looking at the Reformation as essentially a religious movement that only religious factors can explain.

The historian Rambaud presents convincing evidence that the

invention of printing played a great role.[1] The printing press reproduced in mass quantities not only ancient profane classics but an extraordinary number of Bibles as well. Independent historians such as F. Buisson go so far as to say that as many as four hundred editions of the Bible or substantial portions of it had been published before the time of Luther. As a result, Buisson says, the unique and divine image of Jesus Christ was enthroned in the hearts of numberless readers and outshone all other human interests.[2] Protestant historians are more conservative in their estimate, yet they say that before Luther's time the Bible was neither hidden nor forbidden in Catholicism, since the world had had one hundred and ninety-nine printed editions of the complete Bible. Of these, one hundred and fifty-six editions were in Latin which, like the English today, could be read by any educated or business man. Fourteen editions were in German. The first German Bible was published at Strassburg in 1466, the first Italian complete Bible in 1471, and a French version was reprinted several times after 1496. When Luther entered the monastery, he was given a Bible bound, not in chains as some imagine, but in red leather.[3]

"The invention of printing," Luther said, "is the supreme and last gift by which God advances the things of the gospel. It is the last flame which shines before the extinction of the world."[4] This invention made it possible for many common men to read the Bible. As they compared the ways of the Bible with the ways of the church at that time, their minds were enlightened. To them it was clear that the church of the fifteenth century was far away from the church as described in the New Testament. Thus, many people longed for a return to the simplicity of the primitive church. They desired a reformation. A reformation would be a vast and radical change achieved through a series of reforms undertaken by the established and legal authorities. But neither this desire of many nor the will of the authorities brought about the desired change. It took Luther to occasion it. And it happened apart from his original intentions.

Luther was not a practical man. He was simply a monk teaching Bible at the University of Wittenberg in Germany. He never intended to be a reformer. About the year 1510 or 1511 he visited the city of Rome. His correspondence and writings of that time do not reveal any displeasure with the city, its clergy, or even the pope's court. In 1515–1516, Luther offered a course on Paul's letter to the Romans. This course was full of a great pessimism about human nature and yet had a deep religious dynamism. "The Christian," said Luther, "acknowledges himself as both sinner and righteous at one and the same time: a sinner in reality, yet righteous according to God's consideration and sure promise; and because of this, the Christian is perfect, whole in hope though in reality a sinner, but the Christian has the beginning of righteousness, that he may always seek and ask more." For all his life the believer remains at the same time sinner and righteous so that pinched between these two opposite convictions, present unrighteousness and future righteousness, the Christian perpetually turns to God.[5]

It so happened that in 1517 Luther, as was the custom of professors in those days, posted certain theses or topics for discussion, asserting that when Jesus preached repentance he could not possibly have meant the Catholic sacrament of penance. In Luther's time, penance was the main institution of the church. It was the sacrament in which the priest, as the representative of God, remitted sins committed after baptism. What constituted this sacrament was the sentence or absolution of the priest, and three acts of the sinner: contrition, that is, sorrowing for sin; oral confession to the priest; and satisfaction, or penance, for the sin committed. In the ancient and high medieval church, penances were hard: sinners had to stand exposed to public derision at the gates of a church for months, or abstain from eating meat for several years, or say many prayers, or make long pilgrimages. A capitulary or regulation of Charlemagne was directed against itinerant penitents and suggested more constructive penances, such as serving and working.

The Christian church itself had never dreamed of receiving money in lieu of satisfactions or penalties due for sins. But the ancient Germans had a custom permitting a sum of money to take the place of a penalty for crimes. As they became Christians, their custom and idea entered into the church and prevailed first in Christian lands which, to tell the truth, were far away from the sphere of Roman and papal influence. Then on the occasion of the Crusades, since much money was needed, the church saw fit to commute penances for money, that is, to accept money in lieu of the usual penalties, long fasts, and many prayers. The Crusades lasted two hundred years. After two centuries how could it return to the ancient standards and ways of doing penance? Thus the provision of accepting money instead of penalties due for sins remained and became a permanent institution in the church.

At the time of Luther, sales of indulgences, that is, remissions of penalties due for sins in exchange for a donation in money, were a way to raise funds to finance the various undertakings of the pope and the church. Hence, when Luther proclaimed outright that the sacrament of penance should simply be repentance, and that repentance is not an institution but an inner state of the soul, a spiritual process in the individual, a movement of a man's life turning to God and lasting as long as a man lives, practical churchmen took him for a heretic. Luther's idea of repentance, the church authorities felt, would logically displace and even dissolve penance as its basic institution and the chief motivation not only of donations but also of many blessed good deeds and glorious works for the mother church.

Thus a very great dispute arose in Germany. Originally, it was not Luther's thought to break with the pope, but he became accustomed to this idea during the course of the dispute. And in this he was fortified by his large following. Many princes and nobles, who were nearly bankrupt, protected him. On his way to Worms, Luther imagined that he was challenging the world, but covered by the secret police of the Elector of Saxony, he was never in actual danger of his life. Things went so well that when the pope excommunicated him, Luther and his followers were not heartbroken. Though they did not have any premeditated plans, they had to become churchmen and reformers. They carried on the services in the churches, taking out what seemed in plain contradiction to the Bible. For years many had expected a reformation of the Church, and when these changes came, they were called the Reformation. But, properly speaking, the so-called Protestant Reformation had been a religious revolution,[6] because the changes in several German states were brought about by an unconstitutional, newly self-appointed religious authority.

Frankly, what or who this new religious authority was, is a matter of interpretation. The new authority can be said to be the Bible, or the princes who became in fact the head of the church in their territory, or Luther himself. Charles the Fifth, the emperor of Germany, after seeing and hearing Luther at Worms in 1521, was not impressed. As a matter of fact, he said, "This monk will never make a heretic out of me."[7] The emperor remained a Catholic, though clearly seeing the need for great church reforms and always hoping that a general council would restore the church to its pristine glory.

Some German states remained Catholic, others fell away from the Roman Church, but the emperor needed them all, for he was at war with two mighty enemies: the French in the west and the Turks in the southeast. Since 1524, Charles had promised to gather a national assembly to bring religious harmony into his immense empire on which the sun never set. Finally, in 1529, he made peace with France and repulsed a formidable attack of the Turks upon his city of Vienna. The emperor was now free to attend to the internal affairs of Germany. Always preferring an amiable settlement to a brutal repression of heresy, he summoned an assembly of the empire, or diet, in 1530 at Augsburg in Bavaria. He asked the theologians of both sides to prepare their case so that the congress or diet " could put an end to discord, to have all hostility cease, to commit to our Savior all past mistakes, and with a spirit of charity and meekness to make an effort to listen, understand, and appreciate the advice and opinion of each person concerned, to harmonize them, to make Christian truth stand out, and to abolish all that which either party had done or said against the truth."[8] The emperor was a man of peace, full of good will toward everyone, and let us frankly say, not exempt from many illusions.

Luther and most of the princes who supported him recoiled with horror at the idea of revolting against the emperor. But Philip of Hesse had no use for the cosmopolitanism of Charles the Fifth. For Philip, the German nation did not reside in the person of the emperor but in its princes. In view of the coming diet, the prince elector John of Saxony called the Wittenberg theologians to Torgau, in March, 1530. They agreed on a report (called the Torgau Articles) whose main aim was to set forth the purity of worship and religion that had been established in Saxony. Luther, being still an outlaw of the empire, could not go to Augsburg but his friend and young colleague Melanchthon and other Lutheran theologians went.

As they arrived at Augsburg on May 2, they found that their chief adversary, Dr. John Eck, had published a rather dangerous book in which he had gathered out of the Reformers' publications some four hundred and four statements alleged to be heretical. The Wittenberg theologians could not possibly present the Torgau Articles as they were. They had to prepare a more ample statement showing that they were not heretics but were in harmony with Catholics in matters of dogma. Giving up certain controversial matters such as transubstantiation and the papacy, they prepared a peaceful statement that ended, however, in emphasizing the discrepancy between certain Christian traditions and various present abuses. This document was endorsed and signed first by John, duke and elector of Saxony, then by George, margrave of Brandenburg, as cosigner, then by Ernest, duke of Lüneburg, by Philip, landgrave of Hesse, a few other princes, and the mayors of the two cities of Nuremberg and Reutlingen.

The emperor came to the diet filled with a sense of responsibility as head of the Holy Roman Empire whose crown he had just received from the hands of the pope at Bologna. He was anxious to restore the unity of the church. The Lutheran statement was presented to the emperor in two original texts, one in Latin and one in German. The emperor wanted the Latin text to be read, but John of Saxony objected, saying that, as they were in Germany, the German text should be read. And so the German text was read by the Saxon chancellor Beyer at three o'clock in the afternoon of June 25, 1530, in the Chapter Hall of the Augsburg episcopal palace.[9]

Some fifty manuscript copies of this Declaration of Augsburg, all made in 1530, still exist. Melanchthon published it first in 1531. It is a rather lengthy document and it may not create such an impact as do the shorter and more concise creeds of former times. But as Calvin, on becoming a pastor in Strassburg, endorsed this document, it should be of interest to all Protestants to know its essence.

First of all, we may read in the Preface, " This confession of our preachers and of ourselves shows how we have thus far taught in our territories the doctrine founded on the Holy Scripture and the pure word of God " (Pref., par. 8). We clearly see here that it is a question of a confession of faith, that this Confession of

Faith was meant to be founded on the Scripture and that preaching was meant to be founded not on this Confession of Faith but on the Holy Scriptures.

The Augsburg Confession then offers a first theological section of twenty-one " Articles Concerning Faith and Doctrine." In this, its compilers meant to be ecumenical, that is, they were certain that their tenets of belief were in harmony with those of the Christian church of all times and places, yet they were careful to draw a distinction between " the catholic or universal Christian church " (the *ecclesia catholica*) and " the Roman Church." For them, there will ever be only one holy Christian church. And they define it as " the assembly of all believers in which the gospel is taught purely and where the holy sacraments are administered in conformity to the gospel " (art. 7). For the Confessors of Augsburg, the Roman Church is a local church which in itself has neither more value nor authority than other local churches, such as, for example, the church of Wittenberg, but the Roman Church is a member of the universal church with privileges equal to those of the other Christian churches.[10]

The articles on God, the Son of God, the union of the divine and the human natures in Jesus Christ, and even the confession of sins (art. 11) aimed at conciliation. The Confession of Augsburg showed that Protestants were no heretics, and in order to emphasize, no doubt, its ecumenicity and catholicity, the Confession repeatedly condemned the Anabaptists, who believed that they received the Holy Spirit without the external help of the gospel (art. 5) and did not co-operate with the existing order of society and the government (art. 16).

The Augsburg Confession incorporated the deep pessimism of Luther, saying that " after the Fall of Adam all men are born with sin, that is, without the fear of God, without trust in God, and with concupiscence, and that this original disease or law is truly a sin which brings condemnation and also eternal death to those who are not reborn through baptism and the Holy Spirit" (art. 2). Yet we also find here that Christian optimism which is found on the other side of despair about man. The Confession tells us indeed that the word "faith" does not mean merely the knowledge of an event (for devils and impious men have that) but it signifies a faith that believes also in the effect of an event, that is, believes the remission of sins through Christ. Through faith, the Spirit is received and hearts are renewed and put on new affections so that they can accomplish good deeds (art. 20). The Augsburg confessors concluded the first part, saying that "they wished to transmit to posterity no other teaching except that which is conforming to the pure word of God" (art. 22).

The second part (arts. 22–28) concerned "matters which were contested" and meant "to show the abuses which had been done away with" in the Protestant states, such as the sacrificial aspects of the Eucharist, monastic vows, and useless hierarchies. Here, too, Melanchthon and fellow Lutheran theologians, believing that it was still possible to avoid a definitive split between Romanists and Protestants, aimed at reaching religious peace and unity in Western Christendom.

The reading of the Confession of Augsburg made a favorable impression on several Catholic delegates who thus far had imagined the Reformation as a mere conglomeration of godless innovations. Consequently, a committee composed of men from both parties was set up with the purpose of reaching an understanding in religious and church matters. The Catholics at first seemed to make concessions in questions of doctrine to the point that they almost accepted the Lutheran formula that "men cannot be justified in the sight of God by their own effort, merits, or deeds, but are justified freely on account of Christ through the medium of faith" (*gratis propter Christum per fidem,* art. 4). Melanchthon was also disposed to make several concessions in matters of tradition and institutions. But the Romanists were animated by immense pride, which soon caused them to restate all their beliefs in a manner that would spite the Protestants and to set up a Catholicism utterly different from that of the Middle Ages. Thereby they made any return to the Catholic Church impossible. And their attitude stiffened so that eventually even the meek and conciliatory Melanchthon had to surrender to the most evident fact that an understanding with Rome was impossible, and that the religious unity of the Western world was beyond hope of realization.[11]

Yet the Augsburg Confession of Faith remained and stands to this day as the capital Confession of the Lutheran churches. In France, the words "the Church of the Augsburg Confession" means "the Lutheran Church." As for the original Latin and German texts of this Confession, the emperor Charles the Fifth took both of them with him. The German text must have been placed in the chancellery of the imperial court but it could never be found there, and thus far nobody knows what happened to it. As for the original Latin text, it was placed in the imperial archives at Brussels. However, on February 18, 1569, Philip the Second of Spain asked the Duke of Alba or Alva to bring him this Latin text to Spain "so that such a pernicious work be destroyed forever." No doubt this order of the king was executed.[12]

So, the original texts of the Augsburg Confession of 1530 were lost. But in the meantime a lonely young man somewhere in France was caught by the spirit of the Reformation. He was soon to play all by himself the greatest role in the religious history of our modern Western civilization.

VIII

THE FRENCH REFORMED DECLARATIONS OF FAITH OF 1559 AND 1936

In the light of history, it is no exaggeration to say that French Protestantism was born one day between 1512 and 1516 when a man in Paris fell victim to an inward illumination that imparted to him "the knowledge of the dignity of God's Word and the conviction that all that which is not according to God's Word is altogether abominable."[1] This man was Guillaume Farel. But his new conviction did not permit him to continue to teach grammar and philosophy at the Cardinal Lemoine College in Paris. In 1521, he preferred to go to the city of Meaux where its Bishop Briçonnet had called him. A loyal Catholic, Bishop Briçonnet had in mind to simplify religion, to use more French in the worship service, and gradually to educate the clergy and to better the people of his diocese. Like Erasmus and Lefèvre, the Bishop belonged rather to the Renaissance than to the Reformation. To them the Bible was simply a tool to be used in improving the existing church and in bettering religious sentiment.

For Farel, on the contrary, the Bible was ultimate and absolute. Man is not to use the Bible in view of anything. It is the Bible that is to use man, for the Word of God is the revolutionary factor of an entirely new creation. In its light, dead deeds in man die and real life comes in. The Bible creates a new faith, a new conduct, and a new church. Farel wanted a clean sweep of the old and a drastic introduction of the new. He found his ideas incompatible with those of Bishop Briçonnet [2] and Lefèvre. So, in 1522, Farel broke off from the Meaux conception of lawful and gradual reforms of the church and ventured upon a re-formation of Scriptural Christianity all on his own.[3]

A list of the French, Swiss, and Piedmontese towns that Farel visited and revisited would be prohibitive. Impulsive but honest, this Elijah of the sixteenth century preached everywhere he could find an audience — in private houses, inns, public squares, courts of justice, and jails. Farel's courage was colossal. Not only did he remain undismayed in the midst of all possible dangers, but these even excited his ardor. Driven from place to place, he always left some admirers or disciples whom later he visited and revisited. He thus kept his groups enlarging. Farel's perpetual journeys truly laid the physical structure of French-speaking Protestantism. He propagated and established the gospel not only by the spoken word but through books printed in the current language of France so as to minister to even the simplest people. In one single summer (1525) at Montbéliard, Farel produced, first, a treatise on the Lord's Prayer, substantially an exposition of the Christian life; second, the first Protestant French liturgy or manual of worship in spirit and in truth; third, a summary of what a Christian ought to know. In this work, now translated by the present writer and to be published by The Liberal Arts Press of New York, may be found not only the most primitive Christianity re-formed by the inspiration of Scripture but also the first complete exposition of Protestant principles and vision of life ever composed in the common language of the people. This book created the ideology of early French Protestantism. Its success was prodigious. It was often reprinted because, to the early French-speaking Protestants, it had the authority of a confession of faith or creed.[4] Farel's Summary reflects a few ideas of Luther's, though Farel's conversion was prior to Luther's appearance on the scene of history.

If French Protestantism, as a confused movement of many,

owes much to the pessimism and dynamism of Luther, it owes its first definition and organization to Farel. The early Protestants of France were called Biblicists, but they had not yet a Bible of their own. It was Farel who first suggested in 1532 a new version for the brethren. Olivétan had charge of preparing the new Bible, and he called a young man by the name of John Calvin to help him, and even to write a Latin introduction to the Old Testament and a French preface to the New Testament. This complete Bible was published in 1535. A Bible in French was no novelty, for Catholics had had one since 1496. But this Bible sponsored by Farel is significant because it was the daily food of French Protestantism; its prefaces first made the name of Calvin known among many brethren. The earliest French Protestantism was a kind of rebirth of Israel's prophetism. Its first preachers, such as Farel, were too paradoxical to be kept in Catholicism; they had to constitute a church of their own. Farel not only preached through France but, supported by the powerful Swiss state of Bern, he conquered for Protestantism practically the whole French-speaking Switzerland, including the state of Geneva.

Though a small territory, Geneva was an important business center which commanded the great roads connecting France, Italy, Switzerland, and, farther away, Germany and Spain. Farel made his first attack on this city in 1532 but was driven off, and owed his life to the fortunate bursting of a gun that was aimed at him. But he persisted, and succeeded in having the state accept the Reformation and institute public education. But the church had no organization or independence. As a matter of fact, it was a religious and spiritual desert.

Such were the conditions when Calvin happened to pass through Geneva on his way to Basel. He was seeking a safe nook in which to study and had in mind only to stay overnight in Geneva. But he was recognized by a man who ran to Farel to tell him that Calvin, the writer of the prefaces to the Bible and the author of the just published *Institutes of the Christian Religion,* was in town! Farel had long and earnestly prayed God to raise up a suitable instrument. He now believed that God had answered his prayers. Calvin was the man needed in Geneva. So Farel hurried to Calvin, straining every nerve to detain him, to the point of almost cursing him in the name of God. Farel was a terrible warrior of the Lord, and Calvin later confessed that " it was as if God had stretched forth his hand from above to stop him." He decided to stay.

Officially, the position of Calvin was simply that of Professor of Sacred Letters in the church of Geneva. But the Genevese at that time, having just rejected all religious authority, did not have the least idea of what the Christian faith might be. Their main concerns were business, money, pleasure, and sports. In this confusion, the guiding hand proved indeed to be that of Calvin. He wrote the first church regulations, the first *Institution,*[5] and the first articles of faith, but Calvin soon encountered such an opposition on the part of old ruling families in Geneva that any but such a man as he would have broken down.

The first question was that of the Protestant refugees or Protestant cosmopolitanism. It is unfortunate that certain modern men still entertain in their own imaginations a horrible picture of Calvin. As a matter of fact, the Calvin of history was quite different. In personal relations, Calvin was affable, obliging, devoted to the cause of the Reformation, always ready to help a Protestant in need. Calvin invited persecuted Protestants from anywhere and everywhere to come to Geneva. The old Genevese resented the presence of these foreigners. But by keeping and settling them there, Calvin transfused into the city confirmed Protestant blood. The energy of these new men, many of whom had sacrificed everything for the gospel, gave Geneva its true independence. Thus Calvin changed Geneva from a town to a city and from a city to a metropolis that is to this day the capital of Protestantism.

The second great question was government. Calvin never spoke of a separation of church and state. He considered both ministers and state officials as proxies of God. He wanted a theocracy. He persisted. And never has history known a more complete triumph of a discipline. Geneva in the long run was changed. It was no longer the city of vain luxury, of carefree gaiety, and of mocking skepticism. Another city was born: of austere aspect, of grave customs, enlightened only by the exaltation of its faith. Under the hand of Calvin, Geneva was remolded: it had to surrender first its provincialism to nationalism, then its nationalism to a universal mission. The last achievement of Calvin was a great school. With the academy which became a university, Geneva developed as a bulwark against the Counter Reformation, a center of active propaganda, a spiritual metropolis. There, Calvin was expounding the Bible to thousands. And still he was writing everywhere, "Send us wood, and we shall make arrows!" Calvin was a statesman and a man of action. But to act he needed first to know. Without leaving his study, he had his eyes all over Europe. A thousand students, without knowing it, were his intelligence. He was always asking for all sorts of information. A multitude of scholars, merchants, and pedlars were his secret agents all over Europe. They carried his instructions to France, Switzerland, Hungary, Poland, England, and brought back letters, data, and news. France especially interested him: royal displacements, intrigues at the court, rumors of war and peace, plans, decisions, new laws — nothing escaped him. He was the best informed man in Europe. And no one more than Calvin had at heart the unity of Protestantism.

As far away as England, Archbishop Cranmer in 1552 consulted Calvin about making an English creed acceptable to all the churches of the Reformation. Calvin answered that he would cross ten seas in order to do something for the unity of the separated and scattered churches. In this connection, Calvin corresponded with the Duke of Somerset and dedicated his Exposition of Isaiah to King Edward of England. Calvin influenced the Anglican doctrine of the Lord's Supper and the Thirty-nine Articles of Religion whose seventeenth article asserted predestination as the eternal design of God by which, before creating the world and from all eternity, God has decreed to save us. At the time of Queen Elizabeth, Calvin's *Institutes* was translated into English by Thomas Norton and published at London in 1561. Richard Hooker and many Anglicans praised it to the stars. And the Anglican Church came to be a compromise between Catholicism and Calvinism.

Calvin constantly strove for the unity of the Reformation. According to him, the common hatred against Rome was not sufficient to create unity. Union had to be sought first in sacraments, then in all doctrine. By what means? A universal council. But the general council was never to assemble. Yet Calvin succeeded in consolidating the Reformed Churches in the Palatinate, Scotland, Holland, France, and Piedmont. These churches were all scattered, but a mighty common discipline inspired from Geneva held them together and made them able to withstand all adversity. Everywhere individualism, provincialism, and nationalism were absorbed and transcended into something higher. From the Geneva of Calvin went Englishmen, Scots, Frenchmen, Swiss, Italians, Poles, Spaniards, Frisians, Flemish. . . . They went forth from city to city, from town to town; proscribed, dispersed, wandering throughout the world. Yet they felt not alone. A light, far away, guided and inspired them. These men had only one fatherland: their religion; one certainty: their election; one reason for living: the triumph of God's cause.[6]

And when politicians in France were thinking of annihilating "heresy" by the number of blows and atrocity of punishments, they found with dismay that the hydra multiplied itself under their blows. For every martyr who perished in the fire, a hundred more marched forth. Judges could never forget the faith professed by their victims, and executioners were converted to the faith of those whom they had burned.[7] It was not long before France alone had nearly two thousand Reformed Churches. According to Chastel,[8] about the year 1555 there were nearly four hundred thousand Reformed Protestants in that kingdom. They felt such a need for fellowship that they decided to organize even at the risk of their existence.

In 1557, thirty-five members, including several distinguished ladies, of the church in Paris (which at that time had four ministers) were arrested. Seven were instantly condemned and executed. Calvin, in Geneva, made an effort to appeal to the king of France. He sent Théodore de Bèze to beg Swiss city-governments and German princes to intercede for the release of the Parisian prisoners. It was at this time that Calvin, in co-operation with the pastors of Paris, wrote a confession of faith, intended to show to the German princes what the prisoners of Paris really believed. The princes not only failed to move King Henry of France but more Protestants were burned at the stake. The situation was horrible and hopeless when sudden help came from a most unexpected quarter.

In May, 1558, as some believers were singing the psalms of Marot at Pré-aux-Clercs in Paris, some strollers in that park, touched by Protestant courage, joined the singers, and the crowd became so large that the authorities could do nothing about it. This demonstration lasted for several days. The king of Navarre, the prince of Condé and a group of lords joined this mass meeting. Five thousand people came to gather at Pré-aux-Clercs, and the rumor was that two nephews of Montmorency, the commander in chief of the French army, as well as the commanding general of the infantry, d'Andelot, and Admiral Coligny had joined the Reformation. Encouraged by this manifestation of sympathy, which unfortunately was to be temporary and superficial, the church of Paris became bold enough to summon a general assembly or synod of the churches of France so as to set up a church constitution, following the projects of Calvin as the churches of Paris and Poitiers had already suggested.

With infinite precautions, about twenty delegates representing seventy-two churches arrived in Paris on May 23, 1559. The secret meetings were held in a private house in the Saint-Germain borough which already at that time was nicknamed "The Little Geneva." Pastor Francis Morel of Paris was elected moderator of the synod. After four days of deliberation, the delegates scattered, carrying away their hasty copy of the first Confession of Faith of the Reformed Churches of France.[9]

Calvin's draft had thirty-five articles. The French Synod recast the first two and expanded them into six, so that the total confession has forty articles. From article 8 on, the confession did not depart considerably from Calvin's draft.

Calvin's first and capital affirmation had been that "as the fountain of believing is the Word of God, we believe that the living God is manifested in his law and through the prophets and finally in the gospel. . . . God alone gives the certainty of this teaching to his elect and seals it in their hearts by his Spirit."[10] In Calvin's draft, all the following articles depended on this first article. Calvin's original concept and first article were suppressed, and the confession was made to open with a series of declarations about the essence of God as one, simple, spiritual, eternal. . . . Article 2 states that God disclosed himself in his creation, yet more clearly in his Word. In this the synod went nearer to Catholicism.

The Scripture is set forth as the rule of faith and supreme authority, self-evident and therefore independent of man. The three symbols or creeds (Apostles', Nicene, and Quicunque vult) are accepted since they conform to God's Word and to the ancient fathers of the church (arts. 3–5). The Trinity (art. 6), Creation (art. 7), and Providence (art. 8) are asserted. Articles 9–11 proclaim the sinfulness of man, the impossibility of a natural religion, and the necessity of grace. We are elected in Christ (art. 12). He is our deliverer (art. 13) both divine and human (arts. 14–15). His death shows God's love (art. 16), reconciliation and reparation (art. 16), so that we have now peace with God (arts. 17–18). Faith is not our own working but the work of the Holy Spirit (art. 21) and produces good deeds (art. 22).

The confession emphasizes the importance of the church. The true and one church is that where the Word of God is preached and lived in its purity, and the sacraments are administered in conformity to God's Word (arts. 25-27).

To attend Catholic meetings means to separate oneself from the body of Christ. Yet Catholic baptisms are valid (art. 28). The church should have pastors, elders, and deacons (art. 29). All pastors and churches are equal (arts. 29–30). Sacraments are added to the Word of God to evidence further the grace of God (arts. 34–38). Governments are necessary (art. 39). We must conform to their laws, "provided that the absolute sovereignty of God remain intact" (art. 40).

At the Seventh National Reformed Synod held at La Rochelle in 1571, this Confession of Faith was confirmed by all the churches of France, approved and signed by the representatives of three national churches, that is, by Théodore de Bèze for the Church of Geneva, by Jeanne d'Albret (Queen of Navarre and mother of Henry IV, future king of France) for the National Church of Bearn, and by Coligny for the Church of France. This Confession of Faith is therefore also known as the Confession of La Rochelle or the Gallican Confession. It soon had a German translation [11] and an old English version.[12]

The Protestant martyr Guy de Brès composed, in thirty-seven

articles, a confession of faith for the Walloon and Flemish Reformed Churches. It was revised by Adrien de Saravia and approved by the Walloon and Flemish Synod of Embden in 1571. It does not show any significant variation in spirit or thought from that of France, and is known under the name of Belgic Confession — *Confessio Belgica.*[13]

French Protestants still hold the Gallican or La Rochelle as a capital confession of faith and have republished it at least twice in recent years.[14] It is indeed a classic expression of French Protestantism. In 1936 the Reformed Churches of France in view of their reunion, which was indeed effected in 1938, reaffirmed the Confession of Faith of La Rochelle and issued the following Declaration of Faith which we here translate and offer in its entirety as well as its Preamble which, as one may see, applies to the ordination of its ministers:

" French Reformed Declaration of Faith of 1936

" At the moment of confessing her faith in the Sovereign God and in Christ the Savior, the Reformed Church of France before all things feels the need to raise a cry of gratitude and adoration toward the Father of mercies.

" Faithful to the principles of faith and liberty upon which she has been founded, in communion with the universal church, she affirms the perpetuity of the Christian faith expressed successively through the Apostles' Creed, ecumenical creeds and confessions of faith of the Reformation, especially the Confession of La Rochelle; she finds the spring of her faith in the central revelation of the gospel: God has so loved the world that he has given his only Son to the end that whosoever believes in him perishes not but has eternal life.

" With her fathers and martyrs, with all the churches issued from the Reformation, she affirms the sovereign authority of the Holy Scriptures such as it is founded in the inner witness of the Holy Spirit, and acknowledges therein the rule of faith and life.

Confronted by the estrangement (*déchéance*) of man, she proclaims salvation through grace by means of faith in Jesus Christ, unique Son of God who has been given up for our offenses and resurrected for our justification.

"At the base of her teaching and worship, the Reformed Church of France puts the great Christian facts affirmed in the gospel, represented in her sacraments, celebrated in her religious solemnities, and expressed in her liturgy.

"In obedience to her divine vocation, she announces to the sinful world the gospel of repentance and forgiveness, new birth, holiness, eternal life.

"Through the action of the Holy Spirit, she shows her faith through her works: in prayer she works for the awakening of souls, for the manifestation of the unity of the body of Christ and peace between men. Through evangelization, missionary work, and struggle against social evils, she prepares the ways of the Lord until the Kingdom of God and its righteousness shall come through the triumph of her chief.

"To Him who by the power which acts in us is able to do infinitely more than we ask and imagine, to him be glory in the church and in Jesus Christ, from generation unto generation, from centuries unto centuries! Amen!

"Preamble

"Before making the promises by which you are going to affirm your consecration to the service of God and Jesus Christ, the Reformed Church of France invites you to hold publicly to her Declaration of Faith.

"This statement of faith reminds you of the permanent principles of the Reformation as well as the facts and truths upon which the church of God is founded.

"To it you will joyfully adhere, letting it be a free and personal affirmation of your faith. Without attaching yourselves to the letter of its formulas, you will proclaim the message of salvation which they express: thus the faithful preaching of the gospel of Jesus Christ will be maintained, according to the apostolic testimony and in conformity to the tradition of faith and Christian life which we have received from our fathers."[15]

Such is the ancient and modern faith of the Reformed Church in France. Historians especially look at French Protestantism as unique. Basically, it rested neither on the princes, as in Germany, nor on kings, as in England, nor on democratic patriotism, as in Switzerland, nor on certain families, nor on racial reasons. It rested on the Bible. It produced thousands of martyrs, eventually a king, Henry IV, a president of the republic such as G. Doumergue, a premier of France such as F. Guizot, brilliant philosophers such as Paul Ricoeur, numberless theologians, and incomparable writers such as A. Gide, the "frightful hero" who in 1909 took up the defense of the memory of Calvin against P. Claudel. All kinds of men and women are found in French Protestantism. They are the first to accept new truths and the last to abandon the old. To this day, French Protestantism is a fervent brotherhood, a glorious minority that belongs to no party, no political group, no financial clique. What is the secret of such variety of personality, brilliance of thought, warm fervor, and persistent unity? Those who know answer that "it is simply the ancient French spirit that fears nothing except the Lord and bows before no one but God."[16]

IX

THE GREAT PURITAN OR WESTMINSTER CONFESSION, 1647

In the sixteenth century, England had neither industry nor commerce. Its population was made up mostly of farmers and country gentlemen. London was but a town of some twelve thousand souls. When Luther posted his famous theses in 1517, his opinions spread into England with an extraordinary rapidity. The reason was that, in a certain sense, England had been Lutheran before the time of Luther. It was indeed a devout nation, yet jealous of its independence and anxious to keep its money within its own borders. For centuries it had resented the pope's interference in national affairs; and it was weary of monks and contributions. In 1521, students at Cambridge so freely discussed Luther's ideas in the tavern of The White Horse that the latter came to be nicknamed " The Little Germany." By the year 1524, a young clerk named William Tyndale already had in mind to prepare an English version of the New Testament from the Greek. After a visit to Luther, Tyndale sought safety and peace in the Low Lands and from there smuggled into England pamphlets, portions of Scriptures in English, and finally his translation of the entire New Testament in 1526. But in spite of so many favorable circumstances, no Protestant Reformation (in the strict sense of the word) crystallized in England. The reason is to be found in the fact that, as the power of the king of England was practically absolute, its religion largely depended on the king's will. Its religion was to change four times in thirty years.

Henry the Eighth, considering himself to be an expert in theology, decided against Luther and even wrote a book against him. Henry even loved the pope until the day the pope said no to the divorce of his wife. She was the aunt of Charles the Fifth, and the pope feared the emperor. So, Henry declared himself head of the English Church and took a new wife. The Bible came to be used in every church, but the church structure was still Catholic. The king had a few Catholics beheaded because they would not recognize him as the head of the church in England. He had a few Lutherans burned for being "heretics." But other heretics escaped and were to return after his death. Some of the king's advisers were secretly Protestants and educated Edward, his son by his third wife, in the new religion. He had also two daughters: Mary by his first wife and Elizabeth by his second wife. After he died in 1547, all three heirs reigned in succession.

Edward VI, 1537–1553, being quite young, was controlled by his relatives and advisers, who were half Calvinists already. During Edward's reign, Protestantism made rapid headway. To this period belongs the making of *The Book of Common Prayer*—"common" in the sense that it was for "all sorts and conditions of men." And church services were held in the language of the people. Articles of Religion, especially for the English Church as Calvin had suggested, were drawn up. Edward VI died leaving no children. His half sister, Mary, succeeded him. This queen, 1553–1558, was daughter of a Spanish mother, had been brought up as a Catholic, and had even married Philip II of Spain. She reestablished Catholicism. To show her devotion, in four years she burned at the stake over three hundred Protestants, the archbishop of Canterbury, and four bishops. The English people were repelled by this spectacle and all with one accord agreed that never, never again would they let the pope have his way in England.

Queen Mary died without children, so her half sister, Elizabeth, became queen, 1558–1603. Philip II of Spain, the husband of Queen Mary, was disappointed because he had hoped to succeed his wife on the throne of England. Feeling depressed and lonely, he asked Elizabeth to marry him, but she turned him down. Being vindictive,[1] he tried to dethrone Elizabeth, putting in her place Mary Stuart, Queen of Scotland. Moreover, Philip of Spain had a complex against Protestants. He offered to lend his troops to Catherine de Médicis to fight the Protestants in France. He stirred up plots and conspiracies against Queen Elizabeth. In 1588, he gathered the Invincible Armada, an enormous fleet equipped with his best soldiers. Elizabeth had no regular army and could hardly withstand him. With the blessing of the pope, the Spanish Armada sailed to secure the command of the sea so that a Spanish army, concentrated in Holland, might invade England. The Spanish galleys were large and many. A few small English ships sneaked in and cut the Invincible Armada to pieces. The God-fearing English seamen modestly gave all credit to "God who blew with his winds and the enemy was scattered" (*flavit ventis et dissipati sunt*).

The greatness of England was born at this time. Dutch and Belgian Protestant businessmen and artisans, persecuted by Philip of Spain, came and settled in England, bringing with them the arts of manufacturing cloth, linen, and lace. English Protestant sailors, who disliked Philip of Spain, pillaged Portuguese and Spanish ships, and grew rich as corsairs. Elizabeth publicly condemned this piracy but secretly protected the pirates and shared their profits. London became a city of three hundred thousand people. Its many merchants united in numerous commercial companies. The English, who thus far had been a country of peasants, became a nation of industrialists, merchants, soldiers, and sailors. It was these classes who read the Bible, maintained Protestantism, and defended England from Philip of Spain. Elizabeth became a mighty queen. Doing her best for the Calvinists of Holland, Scotland, and France, she became the head of the Protestant parties in Europe. Under her rule, England became a great Protestant power, and the glory of Spain was scattered.

Personally, Queen Elizabeth was enamored of Catholic worship whose display fitted her royal pomp. She favored a church government by bishops as a prop to her throne. But she could count only on the Calvinists. They were devoted to her, for she alone could prevent England from falling under the domination of Mary Stuart and Catholicism. She was unwilling on the other hand to accept Calvinism. Thus it was under her that a special form of Protestantism for England was definitely set up: the Anglican Church — a paradox — a regime of bishops and a half-Catholic ritual with a Calvinistic theology in the middle.

This Anglican half Catholicism, decreed and enforced by the Crown for high political reasons, displeased those Englishmen who, during the reign of Mary, had found refuge in Geneva and in the Reformed cities of Switzerland and Germany. Their stay in Europe had given them a keen appreciation of Calvin's *Institutes,* while their exile had naturally intensified their dislike of everything that reminded them of Catholicism. They returned to England with a Protestant martyr complex. Finding themselves popular among the common people, they now claimed what they called the remains or spoils of papism. They agitated for the establishment of Genevese worship and discipline, which for them was in conformity with the New Testament church. About the year 1559, the English people as a whole observed the emergence of this new class of men, and were sufficiently interested to give them the name of Puritans. The name "Puritan" was well established by the year 1564 when Calvin died. The reasons given for this designation are as various as the dates of its first appearance. Some historians, such as Herzog, Chastel, and Choisy, say that they were called Puritans because of the motto they had chosen. This motto of the earliest Puritans was as follows: "Authority of the Scriptures, Simplicity of the Ministry, Purity of the Churches" (*Auctoritas scripturarum, Simplicitas ministerii, Puritas ecclesiarum*).[2]

This motto was the summary of their whole program. It can be paraphrased as following: *Authority of the Scriptures:* negatively for liquidating all ideas and institutions not clearly found in the Bible; positively as the only rule of faith and life; *Simplicity of the Ministry* as found in the New Testament; *Purity of the Churches:* purification of the church and congregations from worldliness and the least trace of Romanism.

From this time on, we find two religious parties in England: the Anglican and the Puritan. The chief point of discussion was church government. The Anglicans were satisfied. "We have gotten rid of the pope, who was an intruder," they said, "of the mass, which was a superstition, and church services in Latin, which people did not understand. Let us relax and enjoy life a bit. Let the church government be in the hands of bishops: they are a distinct order of the clergy, both in kind and degree different from the rest of the ministers; bishops alone should ordain men to the ministry and be responsible for the doctrine and worship in their diocese — provided they do not plainly contradict the Scripture and the traditional laws, dogma, and worship of the church."

The Puritans, however, having a definite program, objected to everything and anything that they could not clearly find in their Bibles. They would do away with all church ceremonies. Holding that there should be no difference between one minister and another, some Puritans wanted to retire the bishops. Other Puritans, after all, even liked the bishops, especially those who were themselves Puritan, but disliked the pomp and costly ceremonies associated with them. Many Puritans became Presbyterians. The order of events was as follows: Queen Elizabeth had published three laws or acts: The Supremacy Act of 1559: she would be no longer (as her father, Henry the Eighth, had been) the head but simply the protectress of the Church of England thereby clearly and once for all excluding all foreign interference; the Uniformity Act of 1562: *The Book of Common Prayer* should be used in all churches; and finally, the Test Act of 1566: all government officials had to accept and sign the Thirty-nine Articles of Religion. Now, some Puritans were opposed to the Prayer Book because it reminded them of the Catholic Breviary and the Book of the Mass. They absolutely refused to conform to the Prayer Book, preferring to pay fines, lose their churches, and go to jail rather than to use or even see such a book! Being in trouble in the Anglican Church, if not in 1556, in 1566 some Puritans separated themselves from the Established Church and set up congregations that were, in doctrine and discipline, practically Presbyterian.

The resulting persecutions of 1567 increased their numbers and their determination, and made them more Calvinist than Calvin had been. In 1570 there were some one hundred thousand Presbyterians in England. A church openly different from the Established Church was first formed in 1572. State persecution most naturally strengthened Presbyterian hostility against the Church of England and even created a new hostility against the state as state. Presbyterians were numerous among business people and small and large landowners. Their experience under Queen Mary already had led some of them to deny the divine rights of kings and to react to despotism with democratic quotations taken from the Bible. They now felt backed by the Scots, who, led by John Knox, a kind of a second Farel inspired by Calvin, had adopted a Presbyterian regime and even entertained the republican idea of doing away with kings.[3]

Like Calvin, Presbyterians were republican at heart. Because princes, however, were the great force in those days, they did their best to get along with kings and lords, hoping that these would eventually turn to true religion. According to them, the right way to govern the church was by church courts—presbyteries, synods, and general assemblies. For Presbyterians, there was only one ministerial rank. All presbyters or ministers were equal. And to make sure that no bishop would ever sit over them, the constitutions were soon to declare that every Presbyterian minister is a bishop. The distinctive feature of later or political Puritanism was not its severity of doctrine or its peculiar forms of worship, but its clear concept of the immediate relation existing between the individual and God, and its firm conviction that every man was to work for the benefit of his fellow creatures. The Puritan was not his own. He belonged to God and to his country. This made Puritanism a religion of liberty.[4]

Many Puritans, on the other hand, tended to Congregationalism or Independency, that is, they thought that every congregation was an entity by itself; no bishop or presbyter should have any authority over it; the congregations were to believe and do as they pleased. The early Congregationalists or Independents had the illusion that the Bible alone would be sufficient to hold together thousands of congregations into one English national church.

Queen Elizabeth died in 1603 and was succeeded by James, king of Scotland and son of Mary Stuart. In Scotland, he had noticed that the spirit of Presbyterian ministers was not in harmony with the interests of royalty. He openly manifested his antipathy for them by repeating his favorite maxim, "No bishop, no king." As king of England he called the theologians of the Anglican and Puritan parties to a conference at Hampton Court, and himself debated matters with the Puritans.

James was succeeded as king by his son Charles the First.

Charles had married a fervent Catholic, who decided the mode of worship in the royal palace. The king's Catholic leaning and religious absolutism forced Puritans and Liberty lovers to unite more closely so as to survive despotism. Charles thought to do in Scotland what he had done in England, that is, re-establish the episcopate (abolished in Scotland since 1592) and force the Anglican Prayer Book on the Scots. The result was that all classes of Scotland revolted and formed a league called, after the Bible, the Covenant, meaning the alliance of God with Israel. Their revolt was political and religious at the same time. To subdue the Scots, Charles needed more money to finance his army. As only Parliament could pass new taxes, the king summoned the Parliament, 1640. The Parliament, now full of Puritans, bitterly attacked the royal administration.

In 1641 there was a massacre of Protestants in Ireland. The king was blamed for this atrocity, and war broke out between king and Parliament, 1642. On the ground that bishops should not be involved in worldly matters, Parliament excluded all bishops from its House of Lords, February, 1642. In 1643, all archbishops, bishops, and archdeacons were deposed, and their titles abolished.

The Anglican Church government having been done away with, the question now was, Who shall govern the church? The Parliament decided that an Assembly of Divines, to meet at Westminster in June, 1643, should answer this question and advise the Parliament as to the new form of church government.

The Westminster Assembly met on July 1, 1643. Legally, it was simply a body of experts to advise the government. Yet, as the Parliament had appointed two members from every county, the Assembly really represented the nation. Its members were thirty laymen (ten members from the House of Lords and twenty members from the House of Commons) and one hundred and twenty-one clergymen. The latter were Anglican by ordination

served the revolution. Neither England nor Presbyterianism could escape this law in history.

Born in 1599 in a place near Cambridge where religious fanatics were not rare, Oliver Cromwell was a descendant of a nephew of Thomas Cromwell, adviser to King Henry the Eighth. Thomas Cromwell had been the instrument that established the episcopate and the most absolute monarchy in England. And now his descendant Oliver Cromwell paradoxically was to be the instrument of a revolution that destroyed the episcopate and the kingship. To Oliver Cromwell, the ideal man was the "saint." He was convinced that the saints were destined to govern the world. Everything should be subjected to the saints. But to assure the triumph of the saints, force was needed, hence the army. The clear-minded and well-balanced Fieschi, ambassador of Genoa to England, after seeing the army of Oliver Cromwell, reported to his government, "It is an army of monks."[7] Cromwell's army was indeed a religion militarily organized. Each military exercise, each military order and signal, had a Biblical name. Each rolling of drums had a Biblical name: the recall of Saint Matthew would assemble the troops; and the general alarm was named "the call of revelation."

Apparently, Cromwell's master thought was that Catholicism was the greatest of perils; the real cause of the war had been papism. To be safe, one needed to destroy Catholicism. The germ of papism is episcopalism; therefore, to destroy episcopalism, Cromwell needed the Presbyterians; and he let them do it. The universities also were well "purified," that is, in Cambridge alone two hundred teachers had to leave. The Presbyterians were rational, moderate, and the best party. But Cromwell did not appreciate the Presbyterians. More and more he relied on his army and extremist advice. And, as in all revolutions, the moderates — the Presbyterians in this case — were to be overwhelmed by the extremists. The extremists were the Congregationalists or Independents; and their ranks were soon joined by Anabaptists, millenarians, antinomians, levelers, and all sorts of demagogues going to excesses. The moderate Presbyterians were bypassed. The king was beheaded. "The scaffold being cleared, the body was taken away; it was already enclosed in the coffin when Cromwell desired to see it; he looked at it attentively, and raising the head, as if to make sure that it was indeed severed from the body: 'This,' he said, 'was a well-constituted frame, and one which promised a long life.'"[8]

The execution of the king soon proved to have been a great mistake. As soon as he was executed, people dipped their handkerchiefs in the king's blood so as to have a relic. A legend was soon built around the memory of the monarch: the king had been a martyr; he had died like a saint. Once Cromwell had died, 1658, and his son had proved to be a failure, the monarchy was readily re-established, and with it the Anglican Church which, after so many religious excesses, was a relief to the English people.

Because of the caprices of history and the excesses of the English Revolution, Presbyterianism was pushed out of the English national life and soon forgotten. However, it had made its way to the very center of the life of Scotland and passed into the New World. The American Presbyterian churches early adopted the Westminster Confession. The Synod in Philadelphia, February 19, 1729, formally approved it as church doctrine.[9] And the Westminster Confession remains. It is the monument of Calvinist theology which Puritan scholasticism has erected for our study and consideration. When seen in the light of its time and circumstances, and above all in the light of God's revelation and Puritan suffering for that revelation, the Westminster Confession becomes alive and radiant.

The doctrine of Westminster may appear hard and implacable, since it does not give sufficient prominence to the love of God.

But this was, and is, a theology for hard times and dark days. The rigidity of Calvinist dogma will always appeal to courageous, austere, and thoughtful Christians. The words "Puritan" and "Westminster" may be in disrepute among snobs and vain people, but no responsible person can overlook their contribution to liberty and human progress or fail to pay homage to the Puritan concept of human life that consists in knowing God, serving him in life and death, and enjoying him forever.[10]

CONCLUSION

A READING of the principal creeds or confessions of faith naturally raises the question of Christian unity. The problem of Christian unity is complex. First, what about Roman Catholicism? The Catholic religion and Church have been so changed through and since the Council of Trent, 1545–1563, that even if Protestants should go back to the Catholic Church, they would not go back to the church they left nearly five hundred years ago. How are we to go back to something that no longer exists?

As for Protestantism, there are all kinds of denominations and all sorts of individuals. To us, Protestantism means Calvinism. Calvinism, which was a later development, included Luther, while Lutheranism did not include Calvin. Lutheranism remained Lutheranism. It may seem a paradox, but the solid truth is that every Calvinist is a Lutheran, since he has in himself Luther's first contributions; but no Lutheran would claim the name of Calvin. So, as far as we can now see, Calvinism has a bright and promising future.

When we speak of great possibilities, we do not refer to extraordinary numbers of congregations or members. We mean that in Calvinism we have a definite starting place, a great store of ideas, institutions, and learning which in themselves constitute an exciting challenge. Luther was bound by medieval ideas, whereas Calvin participated in and absorbed the Renaissance. Calvin was more cosmopolitan, and from the very beginning, the Reformed Churches included all sorts of races and nationalities. Calvinism is not only broad but rich. Calvin offers an infinity of ideas and answers to innumerable situations and predicaments. Calvin always knew how to bridge the absolute demands of God and the realities of this world which cannot be changed. Truly, his is the most complex and complete of all Protestant systems of thought and life.

Most Presbyterian and Reformed ministers have never been protected by princes and governments, either lay or clerical, and probably never will be. These ministers need patience, endurance, and a sort of personal hardening to adversity that only the rich legacy of Calvinism can provide.

The creeds were generally made to face and stop a danger, so the question arises, What endangers Christianity today? No outside danger is really dangerous so long as we do not let it become a part of ourselves. That day, we are potentially lost. The dangers of today are to be found in our back yards rather than in the Vatican, in the Kremlin, or in the Great Heavenly Palace in Peiping. Our perpetual danger is our own environment. We live in a democracy, in schools and in contact with educators. There is always the temptation to imagine Jesus as a great democrat, the master teacher of mankind who taught plain and reasonable things. The transcendent Christ is a stranger and a foreigner. When this happens, there is an occasion for a requiem for the church — judging from a historical point of view. The perennial danger is that Christianity may be considered as a mere aspect of national life instead of the root of all life. When Christianity has become just one of the many features of national life, it is then already subject to all other features of secular life and consequently suffocated. An indication that in some quarters Christianity may now be dead is the fact that many men and women think of Christianity as something to be found in a near or distant future. As psychology now seeks to find out the essence or nature of man by studying cats and dogs, inevitably some imagine that they shall find what Christianity is through experiments with society or, since groups of men are not easily available, with monkeys or guinea pigs. Is Christianity something to be found in guinea pigs, cats, and dogs? Or is it something that will be yielded by some huge machine after pressing a few buttons? Or is Christianity something to be found in the New Testament writings? Science or humanism? The humanist motto was, *Ad fontes!* ("Back to the sources!"). The position of the humanists was that just as great classical literature discloses the nature of man, so the earliest Christian writings reveal the essence of Christianity. Christianity is *deposited* in the New Testament (I Tim. 6:20) and expressed through the great creeds of the church. Now, a "deposit" is not something invented by our personal genius or intelligence but something that was left us in trust (I Tim. 6:20) and that is found not in animals, which are unable to read, but in the New Testament, which any man or woman can read. Therein gold is left to us and gold we should return to society. But does society appreciate Christianity? By nature, society is intolerant and would never permit anything or anybody to be different from its current ways and mores. It would accept Jesus or Paul in so far as Jesus or Paul would in everything conform to modern ways. Is Biblical Christianity today alive or is it dead? The question is complex. Whatever the answer is, as Calvin said, God never abandons his church but rather brings it to life over and over again throughout all times. The church, indeed, has had several deaths and resurrections in history.[1] Hence, we perpetually need Reformers, not in the current sense of "reformer," but in the original Protestant meaning of the word "reformer," as Calvin stated: "There are times when the true church no longer exists; hence, it is necessary for God to raise certain men in an extraordinary manner to build anew the church which lies in ruin and desolation."[2]

A church may be rich, wealthy, have the biggest crowd and budget, and yet be in ruin and desolation in the eyes of God. True Christianity needs to be perpetually restored. We perpetually need the inspiration of the Scripture. " As neither ancient traditions, nor current ways, nor majority opinions, nor human wisdom, nor conventions, nor visions, nor miracles can take the place of the Bible, let us examine, form again, and regulate all things according to the Scriptures." [3]

These words of the French Confession of Faith of 1559 reflect the position taken by Luther: " We must make a great difference between the Word of God and the word of man. The word of man is a light sound which goes up into the air and soon vanishes, while the Word of God is greater than heaven and earth, even greater than death and hell, for it is the power of God and will remain eternally; hence, we must apply ourselves to study the Word of God, and believe and know with certainty that God himself speaks to us." [4] The French and all other Protestant confessions of faith proclaim the *sola Scriptura* — the Scripture alone is the supreme authority in Protestantism. The confessions of faith or creeds, therefore, like the church whose reason for existing is proclaiming the Word of God, have a derived, a secondary, authority that depends on Scripture. The ancient theologians used to say that a confession of faith was not a *norma normans* but a *norma normata,* that is to say, the confession of faith is not a rule that rules (the Scripture) but a rule that is ruled (by the Scripture).

A further function of the church's statements of faith is to guarantee due respect for the Word of God. Our reader no doubt recalls the fact that the Jews, being perplexed by the variety and multitude of the laws of the Bible, wished to know which was the greatest commandment. Jesus answered by giving a summary of the law which was to serve as a key to an understanding of all the other laws of Scripture. The church's confession of faith plays in the ensemble of divine revelation the same role that the summary of the law played in the ensemble of the Mosaic Law.[5] Hence, the confessions of faith or creeds, according to this Scriptural perspective, are a real authority for us. We pay homage to these ancient confessions of faith consecrated by the blood of our forefathers. We are not in favor of changing the text of these creeds or of writing new creeds to take once for all their place. We do not mean to say, however, that the church should not add to the ancient creeds new statements of policy and beliefs in terms understandable to the common people of today. But we also wish the historical continuity of Christianity and of Protestantism to be preserved and kept vital. A confession of faith or creed not appreciated today may turn out to be meaningful to the next generation or even now to scholars, theologians, and common men in unexpected quarters.

The creeds or confessions of faith are our patrimony, our capital assets next to the Scripture. Being far from bankrupt, we have no thought of liquidating them. Rather, let our comprehension of them be ever increased and evermore applied to the needs of men and the church. "Certainly," says Calvin, "we readily confess that if a controversy arises respecting any doctrine, there is no better or surer remedy than to assemble a council of true bishops to discuss the controverted point. For such a decision, formed by the common consent of the pastors of the church after invoking the Spirit of Christ and the grace of the Holy Spirit, will have far greater weight than if each of them separately were to make a resolution and preach it to the people, or if it were the result of a private conference between a few individuals."[6] However, "there is no bond of church union except that Christ our Lord (who has reconciled us to his Father) retrieves us out of the present dissipation into the fellowship of his body so that by his one Word and one Spirit we be united in one heart and one thought."[7]

As we live today in an aggressive and competitive society and have to be individualistic in order to survive, Calvin's concept of the church as the body of Christ is now difficult to understand. Yet Dr. J. G. H. Hoffmann, a historian equipped to understand the past and minister to a cultured society, tells us that the mentality of primitive Christians was essentially communal. According to him, the fundamental fact of New Testament Christianity (which the Reformers intended to restore) was the New Israel taking the place of the Old. Thanks to Jesus, the Christian community or New Israel had become the beneficiary of all the exclusive privileges of the ancient people of God Israel. Jesus had been the perfect accomplishment of the Jewish Messiah, not only by incarnating in his own person the kingly and priestly functions of Israel, but by triumphing over the dark forces of chaos and death. The person and work of Jesus Christ were the foundations of that new Israel which is the Christian church. This new community, gathered first around the resurrected Christ or later around his great apostle Paul, was not the outcome of some common effort of individual men seeking God. The church was rather the result of God seeking man. Conversion meant becoming aware that God loves and seeks us. The new people of God was made up of "elect" and of "saints." It was composed of the elect because Jesus was the Elect of God around whom the elect were gathered.[8] It was composed of saints because Jesus was the Saint of God (Mark 1:24; John 6:69). The word "saint" applied to Christian men and women is not to be taken as meaning "perfect" or "irreproachable," because Jesus gathered both good and bad (Matt. 13:30) and people of all kinds (Matt. 13:47). The "holiness" meant here was not individual but collective (Heb. 2:11; Rom. 11:16).[9]

We find here a forgotten character of Christianity. Throughout antiquity, religions were a universal and collective fact. They could be located in three classes. First were religions of servitude.

For these, man was a sort of sacred slave whom the gods had created in order to assure for themselves the continuity of sacrifices and offerings. Such were the religions of Mesopotamia. We find then the religions of trial. In these, God did not create man a slave to satisfy the selfish desire of the divinity; yet man after death is to account for his own deeds and to receive either reward or punishment, either heaven or hell. Egypt and Islam might well illustrate this second type of religion. We finally find the religion of deliverance, such as Christianity. Here, although man is also subject to trial on earth, God rescues man out of love to the point that God sacrifices himself for the sake of man's deliverance.

Consequently, these three types of religion place man in different conditions before God. The ancient Babylonian served his gods in order to obtain a happy life, a prosperous old age, material riches, and numerous posterity. The Egyptian honored his gods in order to pass death without difficulty and to acquire the right to ascend to heaven in the luminous boat of Ra.[10] As for Christianity, its perpetual content is the re-establishment of unity with God and man's return to him. This return is conceivable only if we admit a previous separation (which is an evidence of human freedom) and believe that man must co-operate in putting an end to that alienation from God. The man who faces the God of Jesus Christ sees in him a God of love, a possibility that he makes his own by willingly accepting it for himself. If man became estranged in the solidarity (being one) with the first Adam, he can be found, freed, and reconciled to God through solidarity (feeling one) with the Second Adam, that is, Jesus Christ. We find here the only possibility of a moral restoration for humanity and for each individual composing it.[11] The Christian religion, therefore, is a social fact.

Originally, Christianity was a revolution in the pagan world. The principle of paganism was that society is the ultimate goal of all things. We see no principle in pagan antiquity except that man had been made for the state, the citizen for his country. That was an axiom with Plato and Aristotle, and the principle of public law. Yet the final phase of Roman society offers the strange spectacle of being a sort of banquet hall where a few (served by a multitude of slaves) gorged themselves without measure. So that, if we take ancient society by itself and for itself, it appears as the vestibule of nothingness for both the masses and the privileged few. The early Christian churches were scattered in such a Roman world, yet they were held together by a certain awareness and sentiment of solidarity, that is, the sense of being one in Christ. According to Tertullian, the pagans noticed the early Christians' love for one another.[12] This ardent charity was a new sentiment and radical solution of social problems. Riches were considered of transitory value and devoted to the good of all those who belonged to the Christian community.

As the reader can see, the consequences of creeds and confessions of faith are practical. The creed points to the Scripture, and the Scripture points to charity, that is, to loving God, self, and men for the sake of God. We realize, the weak point of Calvinism is that it has never sinned through an excess of love. But in this, Calvinism could be corrected on the base of Calvin himself. In becoming an apostle, Calvin did not surrender his Christian humanism. He certainly wished his followers to be accomplished men endowed with charity. Even toward the end of his stormy life Calvin taught that " the word ' neighbor ' extends indiscriminately to every man because the whole human race is united by a sacred bond of fellowship. . . . Love every man as thyself. . . . Even the greatest stranger is our neighbor, because God has bound all men together for the purpose of assisting each other. . . . The compassion that a Samaritan enemy showed for a Jew demonstrates that the guidance and teaching of nature are sufficient to show that man was created for the sake of man."[13] Paul said that the end, that is, the purpose, of the law is charity — namely, love to God, self, and man (Rom. 13:8; Gal. 5:14; I Tim. 1:5). The same could be said of theology. After all, does God need our theology? It would be presumption to answer yes. Hence, the only alternative is that the purpose of theology is to help man out of his predicament. The Scriptures and the creeds therefore should make a difference in human relations. According to Calvin, "the Lord purposely declares that all men are neighbors that the very relationship may produce mutual love."[14] The creeds point to the Scriptures, and the Scriptures should determine our basic relations with God, man, and society.

The Christian lives constantly before God, not only in the sanctuary of his own conscience, but in all the circumstances of his personal, family, social, and political life. Acceptance of the authority of God determines the basic attitude and behavior of the believer. Prof. J. G. H. Hoffmann, for example, sees the laws of nature not as a product of nature but as ways assigned to nature by God. Nature is not our mother, but a sister in God. In faith, the Christian willingly makes the commands of God his own. As the will of God can be but one, the Christian does not believe in two ethics: one for the Christian and the other for the rest of men. The law given on Sinai is simply the summary of the law that God had inscribed on man's heart when God created him and that God inscribes anew in the heart of whosoever acknowledges Christ as Lord. The Christian follows his conscience not for conscience' sake but because the conscience is an instrument of the sense of the divine that God has inserted in every man. The conscience is a bond between God and man, and a medium of truth. There is nothing to hope from a man who has lost his conscience. The possibility of man's renewal rests with the inner conscience. The fact that even savages and barbarians have some religious sense indicated to Calvin that all men have been created to know God.[15] In spite of division and confusion, the world in which we live is still the world of God.

The hopes of Luther, centering on personal salvation, inevitably minimized social responsibility. Moreover, Luther had no hopes for a world dominated by the devil. In contrast, Calvin had hopes founded on God's sovereignty over the world and on man's reason: "To charge man's power of understanding with perpetual blindness, so as to leave it no intelligence with regard to anything, is contrary not only to the divine Word but also to the experience of common sense." [16] Considering themselves servants of the Lord, the first Calvinists never lost sight of the principle that man is altogether responsible for other men. Consequently, they felt each day a greater responsibility to God also in matters of state administration.[17] We are fully aware that this principle led to intolerance and grave abuses in the past, yet who can suggest a richer spring of bold and joyful Christian action in all the domains of human life? Let us treasure our rich legacy from the past, perfect it in a spirit of charity, and express our hope in a Christian humanism that will render honor and glory to God, and help men to live a happy life in our Deliverer and Lord Jesus Christ.

NOTES AND INDEX

NOTES

Chapter I. Creed, Symbol, and Confession of Faith

1. Latin Ps. 135:1; 137:1; 141:7. Our English Ps. 136:1; 138:1; 142:6.

2. Augustine, *Retractationes* II. 6. " There is the confession of him who praises and the confession of him who sighs." Augustine, *Enarrationes in Psalmos* XCIV.

3. Cecil Delisle Burns, *The First Europe: A Study of the Establishment of Medieval Christendom. A. D. 400–800* (London, 1947), pp. 520–521.

4. Firmicus Maternus, *De errore prof. rel.* 18. 1; Clement of Alexandria, *Protrept.* 2. 15. The word " symbol " was later misunderstood. This Greek and Christian word was taken to mean " conference " (Latin, *collatio*), so that it was imagined later that the apostles themselves, before scattering to preach the gospel, assembled and put together the Apostolic Symbol or Creed to which they agreed to conform in their preaching. Rufinus of Aquileia, *Expos. Symb.* 2.

5. Latin, *regula fidei* or *veritatis*. Cf. F. Chaponnière, " Symbole des Apôtres," in *Encyclopédie des Sciences Religieuses,* ed. by F. Lichtenberger, Vol. I (Paris, 1877), pp. 469–475.

6. *Institutes* IV. i. 1.

7. Tertullian, *De cor. milit.* 3; *Ad Mart.* 3; E. Chastel, *Histoire du Christianisme,* Vol. I (Paris, 1881), p. 135; A. Harnack, *Missione e Propagazione del Cristianesimo,* Italian translation of P. Marrucchi (Turin, 1906), pp. 193, 307–308. In the West, Christ was also called *imperator,* the commander in chief of the army. As the word " pagan " then meant " civilian," the probability is that non-Christians came to be called pagans in the sense of " civilians " in contrast to " soldiers of Christ." A. Harnack, *op. cit.,* pp. 308–309.

8. Rom. 8:26. Karl-Ludwig Schmidt, *Le Problème du Christianisme primitif* (Paris, 1938), p. 58.

9. Augustine, *Confessions* X. iii. 3.

10. Tertullian, *Apol.* 18; *De test. anim.* 1.

11. Latin, *formula abrenuntiationis* in E. Chastel, *op. cit.,* Vol. I, p. 135 and note.

12. Tertullian, *Vocati sumus ad militiam Dei vivi jam tunc cum in sacramenti verba respondimus,* in E. Chastel, *op. cit.,* Vol. I, p. 135 and note.

13. Marc Lods, " Comment entre-t-on dans l'Eglise au temps de Saint Augustin? " lecture given at the Paris Protestant School of Theology and published in its *Bulletin,* 16th year, No. 42 (March, 1953), pp. 27–29.

14. G. Kurth, *Les Origines de la Civilization Moderne,* Vol. I (Paris, 1888), pp. 139, 153.

15. Jean Bosc, " La signification des Confessions de foi et la vie de l'Eglise," lecture given at the Paris Protestant School of Theology and published in its *Bulletin,* 18th year, No. 50 (April, 1955), p. 136.

16. Augustine, *Confessions* X. iii. 4.

17. Cf. J. Bosc, " La signification des Confessions," *loc. cit.,* p. 137.

18. *Semen est sanguis Christianorum,* Tertullian, *Apol.* 50.

Chapter II. The Apostles' Creed

1. G. Kurth, *op. cit.,* Vol. I, p. 146.

2. Einar Molland, " Platonisme et christianisme chez les Pères de l'Eglise " in the *Bulletin* of the Paris Protestant School of Theology, 17th year, No. 48 (September, 1954), pp. 66–67, quoting Justin.

3. Justin, *Apol.* 1. 10. The Jewish Creed is found in Ex. 20:2-3 and Deut. 6:4.

4. Justin, *Apol.* 1. 46.

5. " The seed which contains only possibilities or the imitation granted to man according to his effort is one thing," said Justin, " while the reality in which we participate or imitate according to God's grace is another thing." Thus Justin already sought to solve the problem of the relationship between general and special revelation. His general conclusion could be the starting point of a Christian humanism: " All the truth expressed in antiquity belongs to Christians because they worship and love, next to God, the eternal and ineffable Logos produced by God, become man and made partici-

pant in our sufferings and thereby healing us." Justin quoted by E. Molland, "Platonisme et christianisme," *loc. cit.,* p. 69.

6. The *Iupiter summus exsuperantissimus* of the Roman world.

7. Often in contrast to the simple faith, *pistis,* of the Christians.

8. S. Hutin, *Les Gnostiques* (Paris, 1958), pp. 6, 10, 15, 16, 22.

9. J. Matter, *Histoire critique du gnosticisme* (Paris, 1828, and Strassburg, 1843), quoted by S. Hutin, *op. cit.,* pp. 6–7.

10. Against the Gnostics.

11. Cf. Gnostics' dualisms and Marcion's antitheses. For some Gnostics, such as Valentinus, the emanations or aeons proceeded in a series of couples.

12. Note the word "Gnosis."

13. Cf. A. Loisy, *La Naissance du Christianisme* (Paris, 1933), p. 413; English translation, *The Birth of the Christian Religion,* by L. P. Jacks (The Macmillan Company, 1948), p. 332.

14. Cf. I Peter 3:18, 22. Cf. A. Loisy, *op. cit.,* p. 413 (E. T., p. 332).

15. J. Orr, *The Progress of Dogma* (Wm. B. Eerdmans Publishing Company, 1952), pp. 66–68.

16. Used in Carthage about the year 250, cf. P. Schaff, *History of the Christian Church,* Vol. II (Wm. B. Eerdmans Publishing Company, 1956), p. 536, and earlier in Hippolytus.

17. According to the testimony of Tertullian, *De praescriptione,* 36.

18. "*Lord* Jesus" (I Cor. 12:3; Rom. 10:9) goes back to the Aramaic *Maran;* cf. I Cor. 16:22; *Didachē* 10; cf. Rev. 22:20.

19. A. Loisy, *op. cit.,* p. 428 (E. T., p. 346); J. N. D. Kelly, *Early Christian Creeds* (London, 1950), p. 121.

20. E. Schwartz and Dom Connolly.

21. Omitted by H. Lietzmann as being no part of the original creed on the basis of a creed found on a papyrus and taken as preserving the early second-century Roman tradition.

22. P. Nautin, *Je crois à l'Ésprit Saint dans la Sainte Église pour la Résurrection de la chair — Étude sur l'histoire et la théologie du Symbole* (Paris, 1947), pp. 41, 47–49.

23. A phrase of Irenaeus' evidences this ancient understanding or representation: "Above all things the Father, who is the head of Christ. . . . And in us the Spirit, who is the living water which the Lord gives to those who correctly believe in him and love him."

Adv. haer. V. xviii. 2. 11773A, quoted by P. Nautin, *op. cit.,* p. 48.

24. It goes without saying that the rendering of these Bible verses is that of P. Nautin.

25. P. Nautin observes that when, later on, Arianism sought to make the Word and consequently the Holy Spirit two creatures, it was feared that the ancient way of speaking would favor heresy by allowing people to suppose that the Son and the Spirit had not always existed. So, their eternal pre-existence came to be insisted upon. But what was the truth to be protected except the affirmation that Jesus Christ is from God (*ek theou*) and the grace (*charis*) of the Christian is the very Spirit of God? The Nicene Creed aimed at preserving the affirmation that had inspired the older formulas henceforth to be avoided. *Op. cit.,* p. 49.

26. P. Nautin, *op. cit.,* pp. 41, 47–49.

27. In Greek, *pantocratōr,* "maker and ruler," singular in contrast, for example, to the seven planetary spirits (*angeloi kosmocratores*) of Saturninus the Gnostic.

28. A. Loisy, *op. cit.,* p. 429 (E. T., p. 349), stated that in the Roman symbol (ca. A.D. 150) the addition "only one" (E. T., only-begotten) made the filiation or sonship an eternal relation, anterior to his incarnation by miraculous conception.

29. "Conceived by the Holy Ghost" was an addition later than the Gnostics, but the fact is already stated in the Gospel of Luke 1:34-35.

30. Eph. 4:9. Ignatius of Antioch (A.D. 98–117), Magn. 9. 2; Philad. 5. 9. 2. J. A. Faulkner, "The Rise of the Apostles' Creed," in *Biblical Review,* Vol. V, No. 1 (January, 1920), p. 112.

31. "Catholic" appears first in the Apostles' Creed between 340 and 360. The word was common before to designate the church, first, as really or potentially universal, and, second, as confessing the full faith in communion with the episcopate, as distinguished from heretical or separated bodies. On account of its exclusive claim by the Roman Church, Luther substituted the name "Christian." J. A. Faulkner, "The Rise of the Apostles' Creed," *loc. cit.,* pp. 112–113.

32. "Communion of saints" is first found at the beginning of the fifth century. Dr. Faulkner thought that probably we shall never know the original meaning of this phrase: it may mean "communion with sacred things, especially sacraments, and communion with saints,

especially with those departed and with angels." "The Rise of the Apostles' Creed," *loc. cit.*, p. 113.

33. We find "eternal life" first in North African creeds of the middle of the third century. It was added to our creed in the fourth century to give completeness to the Apostolic Symbol. J. A. Faulkner, *op. cit.*, p. 113.

34. II Cor. 5:17-19; Titus 2:11; 3:4.

35. According to Presbyterian constitutions, every Presbyterian pastor is a bishop.

Chapter III. The Nicene Creed

1. Their rallying cry was *Monarchiam tenemus* — "we maintain the Monarchy." E. Chastel, *op. cit.*, Vol. I, p. 397.

2. In later words, the Sabellians confounded, that is, confused, the Persons of the Trinity.

3. G. De Ruggiero, *Storia della Filosofia,* Vol. III (Bari, 1946), p. 249.

4. Greek, *theos,* without article, in distinction from the Father.

5. In later words, Origen divided the Substance of the Godhead.

6. Greek, *deuteros theos.*

7. *Entretien d'Origène avec Héraclide,* edited by Jean Schérer, (1949): *heteros tou patros,* p. 122, 19. See note 8.

8. *Homologoumen duo theous,* J. Schérer, *op. cit.*, pp. 124, 125, quoted by Dean M. Lods. "Le Symbole de Nicée," a lecture given at the Paris Protestant School of Theology on February 28, 1955, and published in its *Bulletin,* 18th year, No. 50 (April, 1955), p. 143.

9. Theophilus, *Apol. ad Autol.* II. 15, quoted by E. Chastel, *op. cit.*, Vol. I, p. 395.

10. Tertullian, *De pud.* 21. There is only one God but he acts on finite things through his Son and his Spirit (*Adv. Prax.* 9; 2. 8, in E. Chastel, *op. cit.*, p. 396). Tertullian's belief was the inverse of that of Origen: Tertullian admitted the consubstantiality of the Father and of the Son but not their coeternity (*Adv. Prax.* 2 in E. Chastel, *loc. cit.*).

11. A formula of faith, two letters, and a portion of his *Thaleia.*

12. Latin, *Verbum.*

13. Greek, *ex ouk ontōn.*

14. Greek, *pro tou aiōnos.*

15. Plotinus, *Enn.* V. 1.

16. J.-B. Duroselle, *Histoire du Catholicisme* (Paris, 1949), p. 16.

17. Greek *ousia* (from *ousa,* part. fem. of *eimi*) properly means "that which is one's own," hence, "substance," "being," "essence." The essence or substance of God is that which makes God, God.

18. Basil, Letter LII, in Migne PG, XXXII, col. 392–393, in F. Mourret, *Histoire de l'Eglise,* Vol. II (Paris, 1921), p. 50.

19. The invisible things are such things as Plato's ideas or forms.

20. That is, of the inmost being of God. The Son has that which makes God, God. See note 17.

21. Such as Plato's ideas.

22. Text taken from a letter of Eusebius of Caesarea to his flock in Hefele-Leclercq, *Histoire des Conciles,* Vol. I (Paris, 1907), p. 442.

23. Athanasius, *Epist. I ad Serapionem* 24; G. De Ruggiero, *op. cit.,* Vol. IV, p. 18.

24. Athanasius, *Oratio de incarnatione verbi* 17, in De Ruggiero, *op. cit.,* Vol. IV, pp. 21, 50.

25. S. Athanasius, *Histor. Arian. ad monach.* 33–34, in G. Kurth, *op. cit.,* Vol. I, p. 193 and note.

26. G. Kurth, *op. cit.,* pp. 190–201.

27. Hefele-Leclercq, *op. cit.,* Vol. III, pp. 10 ff., Vol. I, pp. 724, 729 f.

28. M. Lods, "Le Symbole de Nicée," *loc. cit.,* pp. 144–146.

29. Cf. Jean Bosc, *The Kingly Office of the Lord Jesus Christ.* Translated by A. K. S. Reid (Edinburgh and London, 1959).

Chapter IV. The Athanasian Creed or Quicunque Vult

1. Jerome, Ep. CXXVI. 2 (A.D. 411), to Marcellinus and Anapsychia; cf. Ep. CXXVII. 12 (A.D. 413).

2. Corresponding to our railway and mail services.

3. L. Halphen, *Les Barbares,* Vol. V of Peuples et Civilizations — Histoire Générale (Paris, 1940), p. 270.

4. The original text has the Latin *inferos.* For the classic man the word *inferi* meant the inhabitants of the subterranean abode of the dead (that is, "the dead") or the abode itself. There the pale souls of both good and evil men lived, for early Christians, waiting for the resurrection and judgment. They were not necessarily separated, but Tertullian, the father of our Western Christian theology, thought

that the good had a foretaste of their future reward and the wicked had a foretaste of their punishment to come. Tertullian called the place the inn of the dead. Cf. E. Chastel, *op. cit.,* Vol. I, p. 448 and note.

5. Here the original text ended. The rest was a liturgical addition.

6. In Eastern Gaul, about sixty miles west of Geneva.

7. French, *Léger.*

8. *Fontes Historiae Ecclesiasticae Medii Aevi,* ed. by C. Silva-Tarouca (Rome, 1930), p. 356.

9. *Ibid.,* p. 397.

10. To this day the Greek churches recognize only the Niceno-Chalcedonian Creed.

11. F. Chaponnière, " Symbole d'Athanase," in *Encyclopédie des Sciences Religieuses,* Vol. I, pp. 678–681. M. Lods, " Le Symbole d'Athanase," lecture given at the Paris Protestant School of Theology on March 14, 1955, and published in its *Bulletin,* 18th year, No. 52 (September, 1955), pp. 186–187.

12. C. Seignobos, *Historia de la Civilización,* Vol. II (Paris, 1931), p. 26.

13. L. Halphen, *op. cit.,* p. 270.

14. Augustine used other Trinitarian images, taken from man's mind, spiritual eye of the soul, such as " mind-knowledge-love " and " God's memory-intelligence-love."

15. That is, in terms of the absolute idealist, God's thinking as having been thought, hence objective thought.

16. Augustine, *De Trin.* 14. 8; 15. 5. Here Augustine sounds like Hegel, but it was Hegel who took some of his formulas from Augustine.

17. *Non est ut illud diceretur, sed ne taceretur,* in E. Chastel, *op. cit.,* Vol. II, p. 516.

18. E. Chastel, *op. cit.,* Vol. II, pp. 414–416.

19. *Tres simul aequales singulis.*

20. Augustine, *City of God* XI, 24.

21. As the Sabellians and Monophysites used to do.

22. As the Arians did.

23. Augustine, in *Psalms,* Ps. 118, *Serm.* XIX. 6; in *Psalms,* Ps. 52:9 and Ps. 145:1.

24. Greek, *asugkutōs,* against the Monophysite teachers who confused the two natures of Christ.

25. Greek, *atreptōs,* also against the Monophysites who confused the two natures of Christ.

26. Greek, *adiairetōs,* against the Nestorians who put a barrier between the two natures.

27. Greek, *achoristōs,* also against the Nestorians.

28. In the East there had been endless discussions about this union: whether it was a union by nature (*henōsis physikē*) or accidental union by drawing close (*henōsis kata synapheian*) or union by relation (*henōsis schetikē*). Was Jesus Christ a man who contained God (*anthrōpos theophoros*) ? or a man who received God (*theodokos*) ? or God-Man (*theanthrōpos*) ?

29. C. D. Burns, *The First Europe,* p. 521; J. Madoz, "Excerpta Vincentii Lirinensis," in *Estudios Onienses,* first series, No. 1 (Madrid, 1940), pp. 65–90.

Chapter V. The Role of the Creeds in the High Medieval Church

1. C. Seignobos, *op. cit.,* Vol. I, p. 339.

2. A. Rambaud, *Histoire de la Civilization Française,* Vol. I (Paris, 1888), p. 72.

3. *Extra ecclesiam nulla salus,* Cyprian, Ep. 73; *Extra ecclesiam catholicam totum potest praeter salutem,* Augustine, *Sermo ad Caesar. Eccl. Pleb.,* in C. D. Burns, *op. cit.,* p. 519, note 1. Burns also gives Augustine's words "The whole world is safe in its judgment" (*securus judicat orbis terrarum,* Augustine's *Contra epist. Parm., lib.* III, p. 24) as being not a test of "truth" but an expression of a single allegiance, *op. cit.,* p. 519.

4. *Commonitorium,* 2.

5. C. D. Burns, *op. cit.,* pp. 519–520.

6. Cicero, "They who diligently perused, and, as we may say, read or practiced over again, all the duties relating to the worship of the Gods were called religious, from *relegendo,* reading over again or practicing; as elegant, from *eligendo,* choosing, making a good choice. *De nat. deor.* 2. 28. The Christian father Lactantius, *Inst. div.* 4. 28, said, "*Vinculo pietatis obstricti Deo et religati sumus, unde religio nomen coepi.*" Cf. Lucretius' *religionum se nodis solvere.* That is, the latter two thought religion to be a bond between God and men. Cicero would answer them that if they were right, our word religion would have been *religatio,* and not *religio.*

7. Cicero, *De nat. deor.* 1. 41 and *Inv. Rhet.* 2. 22.

8. Cicero, *Treatise on Topics* XXIII.
9. Cicero, *De nat. deor.* 1. 4.
10. Cicero, *De nat. deor.* 1. 41.
11. Cicero, *De legibus* 2. 7. 15–16.
12. Cicero, *De nat. deor.* 1. 4.
13. C. Seignobos, *op. cit.*, Vol. I, pp. 324, 285–286.
14. This appears awkward to us, but in this the Romans were quite Biblical. Cf. Job 31:27.
15. J. MacGregor in *Faiths of the World* (New York, 1882), pp. 200–201.
16. N. Turchi, *Storia delle Religioni* (Turin, 1912), p. 467.
17. Cicero, *De nat. deor.* 1. 2.
18. O. Casel, *Le Mystère du Culte dans le Christianisme* (Paris, 1946), p. 160.
19. *Ibid.*, p. 69.
20. Celestine I, *Ut legem credendi lex statuat supplicandi,* Ep. 21, *ad episcopos Galliae,* Pat. Lat., L, col. 535, in C. D. Burns, *op. cit.*, p. 522, note 1.
21. A. Rambaud, *op. cit.*, Vol I, pp. 75, 93, 95, 96, 63, 64.
22. Caesar, in A. Rambaud, *op. cit.*, Vol. I, p. 19.
23. A. Rambaud, *op. cit.*, Vol. I, pp. 200–205, and C. Seignobos, *op. cit.*, Vol. II, pp. 77, 117–118.

Chapter VI. The Waldensian Declarations of Faith

1. F. Niel, *Albigeois et Cathares* (Paris, 1955), pp. 5, 50, and 62.
2. This question and its answer are clear when we recall the fact that on the 18 Germinal in the year X (24th of April, 1802) Bonaparte had made an organic law reorganizing the Protestant churches of France and allowing a stipend to their ministers.
3. E. Comba, *Storia dei Valdesi* (Torre Pellice, 1923), pp. 17–18, 23.
4. Giovanni Gonnet, "Waldensia," in *La Revue d'Histoire et de Philosophie Religieuses* (1953), No. 3, pp. 218–220, reported to the writer by Paolo Ricca, of Florence, an alumnus of Columbia Theological Seminary.
5. S. Morland, *History of the Evangelical Churches of Piedmont* (London, 1658), contains the "Noble Lesson" and many valuable documents. A facsimile reprint of this work can be purchased from the Baptist Sunday School Committee, Texarkana, Ark.-Tex.

6. H. J. Chaytor, *Six Vaudois Poems* (Cambridge, 1930), pp. XIV and XVI.

7. This letter is given in P. Geymonat, *Gli Evangelici Valdesi — Sunto Storico* (Florence, 1861), pp. 38–39.

8. E. Comba, *op. cit.,* p. 73.

9. *Ibid.,* pp. 74–75.

10. Who thus can rest on Sunday.

11. This article and article 6 are statements against the Anabaptists.

12. S. Morland, *op. cit.,* pp. 39–41, and P. Geymonat, *op. cit.,* pp. 154–155. Ours is the translation of the text given by P. Geymonat.

Chapter VII. The Lutheran Confession of Augsburg, 1530

1. A. Rambaud, *op. cit.,* Vol. I, p. 520.

2. F. Buisson in *Histoire Générale,* ed. by E. Lavisse and A. Rambaud, Vol. IV (Paris, 1923), pp. 477–478.

3. P. Fargues, *La Renaissance et la Réforme* (Geneva and Paris, 1936), pp. 106–107; H. Strohl, *Luther* (Neuilly, 1933), pp. 23–24.

4. In J. Michelet, *Mémoires de Luther écrits par Lui-même,* definitive ed., n.d. (Paris), p. 314.

5. *Luthers Vorlesung über den Römerbrief: 1515–1516,* ed. by J. Ficker, Vol. II (Leipzig, 1908), pp. 108, 266–267.

6. F. Guizot's twelfth lecture on "The History of Civilization in Europe"; Emilio Castelar, *La Revolucion Religiosa,* 4 vols. (Barcelona, 1880–1883).

7. H. Strohl, *op. cit.,* p. 206.

8. Quoted by Th. Süss, "La Confession d'Augsbourg," lecture given at the Paris Protestant School of Theology on March 21, 1955, and published in its *Bulletin,* 18th year, No. 52 (September, 1955), pp. 197–198.

9. E. Castelar, *op. cit.,* Vol. II, p. 587; *La Confession d'Augsbourg, 1530,* ed. by C. F. Rosenstiehl (Paris and Strassburg, 1948), p. 11.

10. Th. Süss, "La Confession d'Augsbourg," *loc. cit.,* pp. 202–203.

11. *Ibid.,* p. 205.

12. C. F. Rosenstiehl, *op. cit.,* p. 11.

Chapter VIII. The French Reformed Declarations of Faith of 1559 and 1936

1. *Guillaume Farel, 1489–1565, Biographie nouvelle écrite d'après les documents originaux par un groupe d'historiens, professeurs et*

pasteurs de Suisse, de France et d'Italie (Neuchâtel and Paris, 1930), pp. 104–109.

2. Two years later, scared by a committee of investigators, Briçonnet joined in a condemnation of Luther and even acquiesced in the persecution of true Protestants in his diocese.

3. Biography (given in note 1 above), p. 113.

4. W. Baum, *Le Sommaire de G. Farel* (Geneva, 1867), p. VI.

5. John Calvin, *Instruction in Faith* (1537), translated with Historical Foreword and notes by Paul T. Fuhrmann (The Westminster Press, 1949).

6. P. Imbart de la Tour, *Les Origines de la Réforme,* Vol. IV (Paris, 1935), pp. 160–161, 166, 146–147, 171–172.

7. Henri Martin, *Histoire de France,* Vol. VIII (Paris, 1860), p. 480.

8. E. Chastel, *op. cit.,* Vol. IV (Paris, 1882), p. 116; J. Viénot, *Histoire de la Réforme Française,* Vol. I (Paris, 1926), p. 270.

9. F. Buisson, E. Lavisse, A. Rambaud, *op. cit.,* Vol. IV, pp. 531–532.

10. " La Confession de Foi des Églises Réformées en France," ed. by J. Cadier, in *La Revue Reformée,* Tome III, No. 10 (1952/2), pp. 8–9.

11. Heidelberg, 1562.

12. Reproduced in Quick, *Synodicon,* Vol. I, 1692.

13. It was republished by French Protestants along with their Confession of Faith of 1559, in *Le Catéchisme de J. Calvin* (Paris, 1934), pp. 139–239.

14. See notes 10 and 13.

15. Text given by Paris Protestant Prof. Pierre Lestringant in his *Visage du Protestantisme Français* (Tournon, 1959), pp. 156–157.

16. F. Buisson, E. Lavisse, A. Rambaud, *op. cit.,* Vol. IV, p. 535.

Chapter IX. The Great Puritan or Westminster Confession, 1647

1. Through the phenomenon that we may well call " psychological osmosis " (that is, two parties in opposition unconsciously absorb certain traits from each other) this vindictive trait of Philip's was to pass into the Puritans who faced and opposed him.

2. E. Chastel, *op. cit.,* Vol. IV (Paris, 1882), p. 242; E. Choisy, *Précis d'Histoire Générale du Christianisme,* 2d ed. (Neuilly-sur-Seine, 1927), p. 118. We do not need to go very far to find the true sources

of Puritanism: the words "pure" and "purely" are constantly used by Farel in his Summary of 1525. Then eleven years later, Calvin, while in Italy, had written a treatise in Latin "On observing the Purity of the Christian Religion," which was published at Basel in 1537.

3. E. Chastel, *op. cit.,* Vol. IV, p. 242.

4. Cf. S. R. Gardiner, *History of England,* Vol. II, pp. 487, 489, given in A. F. Mitchell, *The Westminster Assembly,* 2d ed. (Philadelphia, 1897), p. 7, note 1.

5. E. Chastel, *op. cit.,* Vol. IV, p. 245.

6. Luigi Illica, *Andrea Chénier,* middle of Act III.

7. E. Buonaiuti, *Storia del Cristianesimo,* Vol. III (Milan, 1943), p. 161.

8. F. Guizot, *History of the English Revolution of 1640,* last two pages of Book VIII.

9. The General Assembly of 1789 approved a slight revision of articles 20, 23, and 31, which has no bearing on the matters we are considering.

10. P. Fargues, *Histoire du Christianisme,* Vol. V (Paris, 1938), p. 73. For a contemporary interpretation, see *The Westminster Confession for Today,* by George S. Hendry (John Knox Press, 1960).

Conclusion

1. Calvin, "*Dieu ne laisse pas son Église sans résurrection, voire sans beaucoup de résurrections,*" quoted by J. Müntz in Paris *Bulletin,* 19th year, No. 54 (June, 1956), p. 3.

2. Calvin in the French Confession of Faith of 1559, article 31.

3. *Ibid.,* article 5.

4. Quoted in M. Bucer, *Instruction in Christian Love* (1523) (Richmond, 1952), p. 66, note 216.

5. Roger Mehl, *Explication de la Confession de Foi de la Rochelle* (Paris, 1959), pp. 10–11.

6. Calvin, *Institutes,* IV. ix. 13.

7. Calvin's reply to letter by Cardinal Sadolet, last words.

8. I Enoch, chs. 37–71, generally, and 40:5; 62:5-16; cf. 48:7-9; 49:2-3; cf. Mark 1:9-11; Luke 9:35; 23:35; John 1:34, referred to by Prof. J. G. H. Hoffmann in "La vie Chrétienne au seuil du moyen âge" in Paris *Bulletin,* 16th year, No. 44 (September, 1953), p. 77, note.

9. J. G. H. Hoffmann, " La vie Chrétienne, *loc. cit.*, pp. 78, 74, 78.
10. E. Aegerter, *Les grandes Religions* (Paris, 1941), pp. 115–116.
11. A. Gretillat, *Exposé de Théologie Systématique,* Vol. VI, (Neuchâtel, 1889), p. 111.
12. Tertullian, *Apol.* c. 39, and G. Kurth, *op. cit.,* Vol. I, pp. XIX, XXII, 116–117, 138, 142.
13. Calvin on Luke 10:30.
14. *Ibid.*
15. Calvin, *Instruction in Faith* (1537) (The Westminster Press, 1949), p. 17.
16. Calvin, *Institutes* II. ii. 12.
17. J. G. H. Hoffmann, " L'Espérance chrétienne chez les réformateurs," in Paris *Bulletin,* 15th year, No. 40 (September, 1952), pp. 12–15.

INDEX